GETTING
STARTED

GETTING STARTED

STARTED

HOW TO SET UP YOUR OWN BUSINESS

FOURTH EDITION

ROBSON RHODES
CHARTERED ACCOUNTANTS

KOGAN
PAGE

First published in 1988
Second edition 1990
Third edition 1992
Reprinted with revisions 1993, 1994
Fourth edition 1995

Kogan Page Limited
120 Pentonville Road
London N1 9JN

British Library Cataloguing in Publication Data

A CIP record for this book is available from the British Library.

ISBN 0 7494 1596 7

Typeset by DP Photosetting, Aylesbury, Bucks
Printed and bound in Great Britain by
Clays Ltd, St Ives plc

Acknowledgements

I am grateful to my colleagues in Robson Rhodes for their technical help and advice in putting this fourth edition together.

The forms in this book are Crown copyright and are reproduced with the permission of the Controller of Her Majesty's Stationery Office.

The rates quoted in this book are based on the 1995 Finance Bill.

The Author

David Philip is a Robson Rhodes Client Service Partner. He is the author of the *Business Start-Up Checklist* which is published by the Institute of Chartered Accountants in England and Wales as an *Accountants Digest*.

Contents

1
Looking at the Project

Are you up to it?

Before carrying out any detailed work on your proposed business you should consider:

- your personal ambitions and the role of the business venture in their fulfilment;
- the aspirations of your colleagues and whether you form a well-balanced team;
- the market for your product; and
- a realistic strategy to exploit that market.

You and your management team

In the early stages of the business, you and possibly a small number of colleagues will be responsible for all aspects of the business, whether it be concluding a major sales contract or ensuring an adequate supply of stationery. Typically, this involves working very long hours and is very stressful. You may suffer numerous disappointments as you come to terms with an uncertain world. You must be convinced that you are able to cope in these circumstances and that your family will support you through any difficult times.

Financiers such as bankers or venture capitalists will not support a business which has inadequate management. Thus, your business should comprise a committed team with complementary skills. In addition, a significant financial commitment from the entrepreneurs is required by most investors.

Setting up in business is very similar to planning for the family's annual holiday. At the outset you choose the area you would like to visit and then research the pros and cons of the various locations by reference to holiday brochures. Having decided this, you look at the prices and pay a deposit.

9

Then you start planning ahead, buying clothes, arranging for a taxi to take you to the airport, cancelling the milk etc. You would not contemplate the exercise without very careful budgeting and forward planning. How much more important it is to apply the same criteria to setting up a business which is likely to be your sole source of income in future years.

However, for those who are prepared to undertake the planning and control, the financial rewards can be great and the satisfaction in being your own successful boss will be enormous.

The market

The first thing to be considered is the market in which you are going to operate and it is essential that you should have the four Ps of marketing firmly fixed in your mind:

Product: what exactly are you selling and how is it unique?
Placement: who is going to buy your product and how are you going to get your products to them?
Promotion: how will you tell your market what you have to offer?
Price: what should be your pricing strategy?

Marketing your product or service is considered in more detail in Chapter 7.

Your business strategy

You should set realistic objectives for your business and develop appropriate strategies to achieve them. These objectives must be compatible with your personal ambitions and values. Most successful strategies tend to be simple and concentrate on the business's strengths while building an adequate defence against its weaknesses. An over-elaborate strategy which prevents management from concentrating on the key issues is a common failing. So too is failing to define the true nature of your business and its markets. For example, does a manufacturer of home computers serve the market for personal computers or that for executive toys?

Price strategy will be a key issue for the new business. It is surprising how often new companies underprice their products. It is generally unwise to choose a strategy involving high volumes of low-price products. In addition to the manufacturing and distribution problems which could arise, you will be vulnerable to attack from an established competitor by sustained price cutting.

The first project appraisal

If you believe that you can give positive answers to the general questions raised in the preceding sections then you should attempt a written description of your business, a 'business plan', in terms which a financier will understand. In preparing your plan you should invite the assistance and criticism of independent parties and, if necessary, enlist the support of financial consultants.

The business plan should convey the drive, determination and character of the management. It should be stressed that it is your plan and not that of your adviser, and an investor will regard your ability to produce a well-argued plan as a pointer to your other business skills.

The business plan will usually be produced as a first step in raising money from commercial sources, but will also be an essential tool in running and monitoring your business. The key elements of the plan, therefore, will be the amount of funds required and the likely return to the investor. Most of your plan will justify your estimates of these two items.

The content of the business plan should include:

- a short (two-page) summary of the business, its management, its projected activities and the funds required;
- the company's objectives and related strategy;
- the principal activities, products and history;
- the markets, customers and competition;
- research and development;
- the management;
- the basis of operation including suppliers, manufacturing processes and distribution systems;
- major resource requirements;
- financial information, including projected profit and loss accounts, balance sheets and projected cash flow statement with monthly movements for at least two years;
- the principal risks to the business and their likely impact on the funding requirements; and
- the long-term plans of the business.

The financial projections should be as realistic as possible but you should avoid unnecessary detail. The projections must be credible; wildly optimistic forecasts of growth are unlikely to convince investors.

Detailed information which supports the business plan should be included as appendices. These must contain the assumptions which underline the projections and may also include details about major customers and major suppliers, curricula vitae of management and market research data.

Do not underestimate the time taken to raise finance. Bank finance can be arranged relatively quickly, typically within one month. Equity finance, however, may take much longer; time-scales in excess of six months are not uncommon.

Preparing a business plan and raising finance are discussed in greater detail in the following two chapters.

2
Preparing a Business Plan

A business plan is primarily a management tool. It helps you to focus, in a logical and organised way, on the future growth of your company. The business plan acts as a control device against which management can measure achievement. It should be prepared whether or not you require outside finance.

In addition to its internal benefits, the business plan also serves as a vital document if you need to raise capital (described in detail in the next chapter). A well-formulated business plan will incorporate the following aspects:

An introduction to the business

This two-page summary is the most important part of the document; if it does not create the right impression on the reader, he or she will not read on through the rest of the plan, and the effort put into preparing it will be wasted.

This section should be a concise overview of the business and its products or services, including the background of the business, that is, when it was started and the highlights of its progress, as well as an outline of the key roles of management personnel, previous financing arrangements where applicable and the current ownership of the business. It should also include a statement of its projected activities and the funds required.

The business's objectives and related strategy

This section sets out more precisely the targets that the management have set for the business and the way in which they intend to reach those targets. These targets would include, for example, level of sales, profitability and how much you will take out of the business by way of remuneration.

Having set your targets, you must describe how and where you plan to sell and distribute your product or service.

You must explain why customers will buy from you and demonstrate to prospective investors that you understand how your market should be segmented, and that you have the ability to sell and deliver your product or service effectively to the correct targets.

The pricing strategy and policy for your product or service should be explained, and compared to your competition. Show how your pricing approach will enable you to:

- penetrate the market;
- maintain and increase market share in a competitive environment; and
- make a profit.

The principal activities, products and history

Before lending you money, a potential source of finance will want to know all about your product or service and the history of your business.

This section will therefore need to explain the product or service, its key features and its benefits to potential customers. It is always useful to include in the business plan brochures or leaflets about your products.

If you have plans for additional new products or services, describe these, and explain how they will meet changing market needs.

The markets, customers and competition

The purpose of this section is to convince the financier:

- that there is a demand in the market for the particular goods or services of your business;
- that you know your product and the niche that it fills in the market-place; and
- that you have confidence in the product or service.

This section should also provide an analysis of existing and potential customers, the market size and trend, and any competition.

When describing the major customers you should mention:

- who they are;
- why they will buy your product or use your service as opposed to those of a competitor;
- when they buy it, whether the demand will be seasonal; and
- what their expectations are for prices, quality and service.

When describing the market size and trends, you should pay particular attention to the current and potential size of the market, and how big it will be in the longer term, ie five to ten years.

Research and development

In many businesses a large amount of funds has been spent or is required to develop a particular product. In this section you should describe the stage of development of the product, costs incurred to date, and the extent to which further finance is required to complete development, test and establish the product in the market-place.

The management

One of the key factors in whether you will reach your targets is the people involved in your enterprise. You should therefore explain how your business's management team is organised and describe each member's primary role, demonstrating how the managers' roles complement each other. Investors are looking for a team with a balance of marketing, financial management and production skills, as well as experience of the product or service you are developing.

A brief analysis of each key manager should be included in which you describe each individual's duties and responsibilities, career highlights, and significant past accomplishments that demonstrate ability for the tasks that will be required.

The basis of operation

A potential investor in your business will also want to know how you plan to operate your business, who your suppliers are and what they supply, alternative sources of supply where possible, manufacturing processes where applicable, including supply and maintenance of plant and equipment, distribution and accounting systems.

This is an opportunity to show that you are in control of the input to your business, and that you have the organisation and capacity to meet the sales targets that you have set. A business which is capable of generating a demand for its products or services must also be able to supply the demand or the door is wide open for a competitor to fill the gap.

Major resource requirements

It is to be hoped that the preceding sections of your business plan have enthused the potential investor so that he or she feels that you have a business and a management team worth investing in. This is the time to go into greater detail on the finance required, the reasons for it and the time-scale over which the funding is required, so as to set the scene into which the detailed figures of the next section of the plan will slot into place.

Financial information

The business plan should include the following financial information:

- projected profit and loss statements;
- cash flow forecasts;
- projected balance sheets;
- break-even analysis.

Profit and loss statement
The first task of a potential entrepreneur is to prepare a projected profit and loss statement to determine that the business is actually capable of producing a profit. It must reflect your assumptions and plans, which must be stated in detailed notes.

The projected profit and loss statement (Appendix 2) can take various forms, but will usually be drawn up on a monthly basis and will include:

- sales forecasts, both by units (if appropriate) and value;
- estimates of the cost of purchasing the goods and services required, not only to meet your sales forecast but also to build up stocks of your products to service future sales;
- salary levels based on projected manpower levels and costs. Included here would be your own remuneration; and
- expenses: that is, all costs incidental to deriving income, eg rent, rates, light, heat, telephone, stationery.

It is essential not to underestimate the level of your expenses; while it may impress the potential investor initially, it will in due course lead to cash shortages in the business.

When formulating your initial business plan, you should prepare the forecast profit and loss statement for at least two years, preferably longer.

Cash flow forecast
The second step is to prepare a cash flow forecast (Appendix 3). The effective management of cash is a vital part of every business activity. The timing of receipts and payments is very important. Management must be

able to anticipate any shortfall and ensure that there are sufficient sources of finance to cover it.

A typical cash flow forecast would include the following:

- amounts receivable from customers for sales. The important element here is not when the sale is made but when the cash is expected to be received, eg 60 days later;
- amounts to be spent on materials linked to the projected purchases and stockholding requirements;
- salary payments including payment of income tax withheld from wages under the Pay As You Earn system and National Insurance contributions;
- expenses: insurance may be paid once a year, rates every month and so on;
- capital expenditure requirements should be phased into the forecast, remembering that heavy expenditure is usually required at the beginning of the project before production can begin and sales can be generated. The capabilities of the capital equipment must be considered in formulating the overall sales plan and related projected requirements and, if necessary, further capital expenditure should be phased into the cash flow forecast;
- the cash flow forecast should include interest payments on borrowed money. This can be a significant expense and should not be overlooked. Any loan repayments must also be included in the cash flow;
- Value Added Tax payments should be incorporated into this forecast as well as income tax or corporation tax payments, as appropriate.

A very careful review is required to ensure that all likely expenses are built into the budget and cash flow forecasts.

It is important to state clearly the assumptions built into your forecasts about things like inflation, interest rates and foreign currency fluctuations that you have made when preparing your forecast and projections. For example, you may assume that the rate of interest on your overdraft is 10 per cent per annum. If, subsequently, this goes up or down, you will know immediately that you may need more cash or alternatively have more than projected. The assumption would be extended to other receipts and payments, such as how quickly you will get your money from your customers and how quickly you will pay your suppliers etc.

Balance sheet
A balance sheet is like a snapshot of where you stand now. It will list your assets and your liabilities and the extent to which you have invested in the

business. It is important, when preparing budgeted profit and loss accounts and cash flows, also to project what your position will be in future periods and prepare projected balance sheets (Appendix 4). This will demonstrate to the potential investor the strengths (and weaknesses) of your business in months to come.

Break-even analysis

The preparation of the budgeted profit and loss account will enable you to determine what is your 'break-even point'. In simple terms the break-even point is where the income from your sales is equal to your expenditure on purchases, rent, rates, light and other overheads: in other words where you make neither profit nor loss. This is a very effective management tool even for those with no financial background. For example, suppose, to break even, your sales need to be £10,000 per week. Then sales of £9000 will mean you are making a loss, and sales of £11,000 a profit. In Chapter 8 we give a more detailed analysis of the calculations of the break-even point.

It is always useful to prepare a very 'rough' budget and cash flow to begin with and then start to analyse and refine each figure until you arrive at an acceptable result.

Principal risks

It is important to understand the dynamics of what makes your business tick. In order to do this you should ask yourself 'what if?' For example, what if sales are higher or lower than predicted? What if I do not collect from the debtors in 60 days? What if a major customer takes his or her orders elsewhere? By calculating the effect of these questions on your forecasts (known as *sensitivity analysis*) you will be in a better position to know what defensive action you can take if a problem arises.

The business plan should go on to describe the inherent risks to which your business is vulnerable and how you intend to monitor and control them. Your financial projections should include the sensitivity analyses mentioned above, highlighting how your profit and cash flow forecasts will be affected by, for example:

- deviations from forecast sales;
- any change in the cost of sales;
- the timing of large expenditure on capital items;
- any possible changes in the pricing policy;
- any changes in the distribution policy;

- fluctuations in interest rates;
- where the business trades outside the UK, any foreign exchange fluctuations.

The long-term plans of the business

This is an opportunity to set objectives for your business in the medium to long term, based on your forecasts and projections in the short term.

Once you have made all your plans, forecasts and projections, and when your business plan has been prepared, you have a document which identifies the level of finance you require. The next step is to determine which of the many sources of finance available is appropriate.

Detailed information

Finally you will need to include in appendices all the detailed information on your business plan. These would include the detailed budgeting schedules, assumptions, details of management, product literature etc. A suggested contents list for a business plan is given in Appendix 1.

3
Financing the Business

Having decided the level of finance you require it is then necessary to determine the structure of that finance and to understand the particular requirements of the financier. Whether finance is required for a start-up, to buy out an existing business, expand the business by increasing the overdraft or on long-term loans for capital purposes, the principles are the same. Most people raising finance for the first time automatically think of their bank and tend to approach their bank manager without really understanding the various types of finance or the fact that there are alternative sources.

Equity/debt finance

A firm's capital can be broadly classified either as (a) equity (shareholders' funds in the case of a company, or proprietor's funds in the case of a sole trader or partnership); or (b) as debt.

Equity
Equity is how much money you and other investors have put into the business. In the case of a company the shareholders cannot, easily, extract their funds from the business except under certain circumstances (eg if the company is wound up or special types of shares are held). While in relation to sole traders and partnerships the funds can be more easily withdrawn, it is not advisable to do so if such an action will be detrimental to the business.

Debt finance
Debt finance is basically the amount of money borrowed by the business where the lender ultimately expects repayment. The period over which such funds are repaid can be short term (eg overdrafts), medium term (eg

20

loans for three to ten years) or longer term depending on the purpose to which the money is put.

Generally, no interest is payable on equity finance but debt finance is subject to the payment of interest on a regular basis.

The relationship between equity and debt finance is extremely important to the survival of the business and is an area that a potential investor will wish to review in detail. As a very general rule you should work on the basis that no investor would wish to have more money in the business than the proprietor.

Financial stability

If it is to flourish, a firm should have an adequate equity base. This can be measured by what is known as the capital gearing, ie the proportion of borrowed money to equity capital. Every firm is different but it should not be difficult for an individual firm to establish within what range its gearing ratio should normally fall. A deteriorating gearing ratio may be an indication that the business is under strain and a further injection of equity is desirable.

The chief dangers of high capital gearing (ie having too much borrowed money in the business) are that earnings may be insufficient to cover interest payments and that cash flow may be insufficient to fund capital repayments. A well-used criterion is whether net trading profits (before interest and tax) cover interest charges at least twice over.

The capital gearing and interest cover ratios just mentioned are not definitive criteria, and much will depend on the efficiency and prospects of the firm. Thus, if the management is failing to maximise the earning potential of the firm's assets, it may be wise to avoid borrowing and instead maintain a high proportion of equity in the firm's capital structure. Similarly, the repayment structure of a firm's existing debt must be considered. Thus, an unbalanced debt structure may be characterised by large borrowings 'locked in' at high interest rates, or by a large proportion of debt requiring early repayment. Until more appropriate terms can be arranged, it would be prudent to maintain a larger than average equity base.

Banks are now far more cautious about lending to risky businesses. They will look for commitment from the proprietors by reference to the level of equity injected and often by personal guarantees. In addition, they will want a charge over the business assets, if appropriate.

To summarise, while the securing of adequate finance can be a major hurdle for any new business, the ability to strike the right balance between shareholders' funds and borrowings can be crucial to its eventual success. The funding of any business should enable it to survive the possible, rather than the planned, outcome.

The next section describes a number of sources of finance, but it is important that a business does not try to use too many sources simultaneously. Difficulties can arise when a large number of lending institutions are involved with a single company, and an enormous amount of time can be spent negotiating and keeping the sources appraised of how the business is progressing.

Types of finance

Types of finance can be categorised into the following broad headings: short-, medium- and long-term finance.

Short-term finance
The term is used here to describe finance for periods of up to three years. Such finance is used mostly for the following purposes:

- to meet fluctuations in the working capital requirements of the business; that is, the cash that is required to meet day-to-day expenditure, such as purchases, wages, overheads less cash received, for example from sales;
- to finance seasonal peaks and troughs in trade;
- for investment in fixed assets with a relatively short working life, such as motor vehicles;
- to act as bridging finance until more permanent finance is arranged.

Overdrafts
A bank overdraft is the most widely used type of short-term finance. Overdrafts, which is the term for flexible, variable lines of credit, are still the most popular form of short-term finance. Legal documentation is at a minimum with these arrangements; interest is often charged at a higher rate than on medium-/long-term loans. However, bank overdrafts are repayable on demand, and are therefore not a suitable way to finance expenditure where the benefits from it are in the longer term.

Trade credit
It is usual for a firm to add to its short-term working capital by making use of the trade credit that suppliers extend. However, to make payments beyond the period stipulated could result in a withdrawal of goods on credit by the supplier.

Customer financing
This method of short-term finance involves a company asking its customers to finance all or part of a contract by way of deposit or advance payment.

Credit factoring
Factoring is another widely used facility whereby the 'factor' purchases the trade debtors of the company for an agreed reward. The advantages here can be improved short-term cash flow and less administrative time spent on credit control.

Hire purchase
Hire purchase is a method of purchasing assets by instalments. After making an initial down payment, and paying regular fixed amounts over an agreed period, a business acquires ownership of the goods. Technically, the financier continues to own the asset until the hirer, at the end of the repayment period, exercises his or her option to purchase.

Leasing
A lease is a means of financing the use of an asset and not its purchase. It is frequently used to finance motor vehicles, office equipment such as computers, photocopiers, telex or facsimile machines, as well as factory plant and equipment. The leasing company retains ownership of the asset and claims any available grant and tax allowance. These are reflected in the rental charge to the user.

Leasing finance may be classified as short- or medium-term finance depending on the length of the lease.

Bill finance
Bills of exchange are a source of short-term money which are used mostly in the export and import trade. A bill of exchange is in effect a form of post-dated cheque which can be sold at a discount for cash. A seller of goods draws up a bill which is then either accepted by the buyer (a trade bill) or by a bank (a bank bill). The businessperson selling the goods can thus turn the sale into cash very quickly by having the bill discounted, that is by selling it to a third party for cash for slightly less than its face value. The buyer of the goods benefits in that, depending on the payment date of the bill, he or she does not have to pay for the goods until they are delivered.

Bill finance, like other forms of short-term funds, may be useful when conditions for obtaining long-term funds tend to be difficult, but bills should not be heavily relied on for this purpose.

Export finance

For exports from the UK it is recognised that there may be a problem with cash collection, or at least prompt cash collection, in some countries. The Export Credits Guarantee Department provides assistance to exporters by:

(a) insuring exporters against the risk of non-payment; or
(b) providing unconditional guarantees of repayment to banks.

Similar facilities are now offered by some financial institutions in the private sector.

Medium-term finance

Finance that has a three- to ten-year repayment period is often called medium-term finance. It is obtainable in a number of forms, with varied uses and repayment patterns. The major uses of medium-term finance are as follows:

- to finance the purchase of assets with a corresponding life, such as plant and machinery;
- to replace a persistent overdraft;
- to provide the initial working capital requirements of the business.

Term loans

Bank loans are the most significant form of medium-term finance with fixed advances being made, usually on a secured basis. Loans are typically made to help firms acquire assets, and repayment is usually spread over the life of the asset, matching the income generated from the asset with the repayments of the loan.

European loans

Medium-term loans are available from certain institutions of the European Community.

Loan Guarantee Scheme

If funds are not available through conventional sources, a firm may qualify for a loan under the government Small Firms Loan Guarantee Scheme. Under this scheme the government will guarantee 70 per cent of the value of eligible term loans to small firms by the lenders (usually the clearing banks) participating in the scheme. Guarantees are available if the borrower is in an eligible business, the proposed business activity qualifies, and the loan itself is for an approved purpose. Eligible firms consist basically of small firms. The Department of Trade and Industry (DTI) will decide whether a firm is eligible in this respect. Most sectors of the economy involving tradeable goods and services are regarded as qualifying activities.

Loans may be from two to seven years with the possibility of a capital repayment holiday of up to two years. The maximum which may be borrowed under the scheme is £100,000.

Long-term finance

Long-term finance normally refers to equity finance and sums borrowed for periods exceeding ten years. The major uses of long-term finance are as follows:

- to fund the acquisition of fixed assets with a long working life such as the purchase or construction of buildings;
- to provide semi-permanent working capital;
- to finance corporate acquisitions.

Equity and venture capital

Most businesses begin with an individual or individuals providing the initial equity capital from their own resources. A potential investor will expect the proprietor to inject sufficient equity to provide a basis for a viable business, and to indicate his or her commitment to that business. This often involves raising personal finance by pledging existing assets as security (eg a second mortgage on the proprietor's home).

However, apart from this source, a number of venture capital and other investment institutions specialise in the provision of start-up capital. Established public companies, too, may provide part of the capital needed to start a business if it is going to produce a product or service that will be useful to them.

Equity investments have been given an incentive by the introduction of the concept of the Venture Capital Trust (VCT) whereby the Government is encouraging investment in unquoted companies. Investors in VCTs will gain generous tax incentives which can substantially reduce the cost of investment and therefore increase the potential return on them. VCTs will be quoted on the Stock Exchange and at least 70 per cent of their investments will have to be in unquoted trading companies with not more than 15 per cent in any one company or group of companies. (This is based on the 1995 Finance Bill.)

Long-term borrowings

Since commercial lenders will often restrict the granting of term loans for periods in excess of ten years to borrowers with proven track records and sound future prospects, we will confine our attention here to mortgage loans.

Mortgage loans are used for the purchase of specific assets such as land and buildings, the assets themselves being pledged as security to the lender. Such loans can extend to up to 35 years and while most institutional lenders prefer a lower limit of some £50,000, special mortgage schemes for as little as £5000 can be found. It should be noted that lenders will only advance a proportion of the cost of the asset being acquired.

Public sector finance

In addition to the foregoing types of finance, a wide range of central and local government incentives is available to companies of all sizes. The following are the main types of assistance:

National investment support

The government gives financial support for investment throughout the UK in a variety of ways. These include grants to study and implement new technology projects, grants to ease the cost of introducing quality assurance procedures, capital and industrial building allowances, and the provision of guarantees to commercial lenders under the Loan Guarantee Scheme.

Regional investment support

As part of its package of investment support, particular emphasis is given to the development and expansion of businesses in areas of high unemployment and industrial decline. These are the 'assisted areas', and assistance can take the form of regional development grants, regional selective assistance, in-plant training schemes and regional loans from the European Community.

Training and labour redevelopment support

The Department of Employment (DoE) and the Training Agency provide a range of schemes and services for the training and redevelopment of labour, and the development of work opportunities and experience for school-leavers and the long-term unemployed.

Small firms support

The Department of Employment's Small Firms Division co-ordinates and implements policy towards small firms. A wide range of information to assist small businesses is published by the Department.

Inner urban area support

These areas can often present special problems, and the government has therefore established a number of areas where industrial activity is encouraged by the offering of tax and loan incentives and the reduction or simplification of reporting and administrative requirements.

Other support
The support given by national and local government is extremely varied in range and depth and often depends on the location of the business. For example, there are grants available in South Wales to encourage the growth of local businesses, which would not be available in the South East of England. It is essential in setting up a business to talk to the government agencies in your local area about what may be available. Appendix 9 contains useful contacts and addresses.

Sources of finance

The sources of finance generally available are summarised below:

Short-term finance

- Clearing banks
- Merchant banks
- Other British and foreign banks
- Finance houses
- Discount houses
- Factoring companies
- Leasing companies.

Medium-term finance

- Clearing banks
- Merchant banks
- Other British and foreign banks
- Finance houses
- Leasing companies
- Venture capital and other specialist investment institutions
- Public sector agencies.

Long-term finance

- Clearing banks
- Merchant banks
- Insurance companies
- Pension funds
- Venture capital and other specialist investment institutions

- Other British and foreign banks
- Public sector agencies.

Equity capital

- Venture capital and other specialist investment institutions
- Investment trust companies
- Pension funds
- Insurance companies
- Public sector agencies
- Merchant banks.

Negotiating the finance

Presenting a case for finance to an outside party can be thought of in terms of a number of distinct stages; each step must be passed before the financing proposal can proceed to the next stage. The approach adopted by a venture capitalist (providing equity finance) is different from that used by a clearing bank (providing overdraft and term loans). However, both providers will base their decisions on a good business plan well presented by competent management. Ultimately they will ask themselves if the business is viable or not!

Venture capital

A business plan and other relevant documentation must be sent to the lender or investor in advance of a meeting. As this is a very impressionable stage, it is recommended that such documents are neat and comprehensive.

The second stage is to attend a preliminary meeting with the prospective financier. This is a crucial stage as here the lender/investor will be able to assess the commitment, enthusiasm and business acumen of the individual or individuals presenting the case.

If the lender/investor gains a favourable impression of the sponsors, he or she will then go on to evaluate the purpose and terms of the business's financing requirements. If the proposal is deemed to be too risky relative to the return on the investor's money, the scheme will be rejected.

The next phase is likely to involve another round of interviews, to evaluate further the prospects of the business. Specifically, such factors as the unique aspects of the business, the likely future environment in which the company will be operating and the strengths and weaknesses of the business will be measured against the investor's or lender's own in-house lending criteria.

The investor/lender, if satisfied with the result of these interviews, will then proceed to have the company's projections closely scrutinised. This will include deriving some important ratios such as the gearing levels, the potential for liquidity, solvency, profitability and balance sheet strength.

At this stage, the sponsors will appreciate how they and their business ideas are perceived by the potential investor, and how risky the venture is considered to be by the investor/lender in terms of:

- the size of the expected return;
- when the return will materialise;
- how certain the return is; and
- how secure the basic investment/loan is.

It is at this point that the proprietor has to consider how much equity the venture capitalist may require in return for his or her investment, and proceed not to give away any more than is necessary in the ensuing negotiations.

Equity backers want only a minority stake in a company; they do not want to end up controlling or owning the business. They usually want capital growth rather than a regular flow of dividend income, and they certainly want the probability of an exit; in other words the prospect of being able to sell their shares either on a quoted market or in some other way some years ahead. Different equity investors have different expectations with regard to their management involvement in the business. Those seeking an active role will probably be less demanding in the negotiating procedure than those who wish to take a more passive role, in the belief that the company will be able to make good its promises.

Many proprietors are concerned at giving up equity in their business but it is better to own 80 per cent of a company which has the potential to grow than 100 per cent of a stagnant business.

Clearing banks

Most entrepreneurs see the clearing bank as the first port of call when establishing a business or looking for funds for expansion. The banks recognise that there is a growing need for them to provide not only finance which is extensive both in range and type but also sound commercial advice to their customers. Hence, in recent years, the clearing banks have established centres (either branches or distinct units) where corporate expertise can be concentrated to the benefit of the customer.

Many people approach a bank manager on the basis that the money is there for the asking. However,.it is important to realise that the manager is acting as a trustee for the bank's shareholders and depositors. The banker will want to know when he will get his money back and that during the period of the loan he can earn his predetermined return (interest). Thus, his prime consideration is the cash flow; that is, will the business generate sufficient cash to meet its debts as and when they fall due, pay the interest on the borrowings and meet loan repayments, again as and when they fall due?

By and large the clearing banks are not in the risk business and the manager will be looking for adequate security to support the bank lending.

The main information required by the bank manager will be your business plan which should be sent in advance of any meeting. At the meeting the manager will appraise the management of the business and its ability to implement the plans as presented.

The level of finance required will very much determine whether or not the bank manager is able to give you a decision at that meeting. Each manager has a predetermined lending level above which it is necessary to refer the proposal to more senior personnel in the bank. It may therefore be necessary to attend further meetings or provide additional information before a decision is made.

The bank will be looking for security to cover its lending to the business. With reference to the proprietor it may require a personal guarantee and/ or a charge over personal assets (such as the home). The bank may also require a charge (debenture) over the company's assets which will give it priority over other creditors if the business should fail. It is essential to take professional advice before completing any legal documentation required by the bank.

To summarise: the raising of finance can be long and frustrating. Good preparation and a sound business plan will greatly enhance your ability to attract funds. If you are turned down by one source of finance, do not give up as your proposal may appeal to and fit the criteria of another lender.

4
Structuring the Business

Before you start trading, you must decide what legal form your business will take as this affects taxation and the accounting records you are required to keep. The four main forms of business organisation in the United Kingdom and their principal characteristics are as follows:

Sole trader

- You are the sole owner of the business.
- You are personally liable for all business debts.
- You can start trading whenever you like.
- No statutory requirements govern the format of the accounting records.
- There is no need to have annual accounts audited.
- There are no legal formalities to complete before commencing to trade.
- You may be required to register for Value Added Tax (VAT) and Pay As You Earn (PAYE) purposes and maintain records sufficient to make the necessary returns.
- You will be required to submit accounts and tax computations to the Inland Revenue.

Partnerships

- You own the business jointly with one or more people.
- Each partner is personally liable for all the firm's business debts.
- A partnership, like a sole trader, has the advantage of secrecy in that it is not obliged to publish its accounts or have them audited.
- Similar requirements to a sole trader with reference to VAT and PAYE.
- A partnership may be created without any legal formalities, as the

provisions of the Partnership Act 1890 will be taken as the partnership agreement. However, it is usual to draw up an agreement at the start of trading; otherwise a successful working arrangement may be spoilt by disagreement over such basic issues as:

- profit-sharing arrangements;
- partners' drawings;
- capital contributions;
- voting rights;
- admitting or expelling a partner;
- withdrawal from the partnership.

Limited company

- The most common form of business entity.
- A limited company (incorporated under the Companies Acts) is a separate legal entity from the shareholders and directors. It may contract, sue and be sued in its own name and capacity.
- The shareholders are not liable for the company's debts beyond the amount remaining unpaid on the shares or beyond any amount guaranteed to a third party (such as a bank).
- Incorporation also involves the preparation of accounts for the company, and having these and the accounting records audited. This must be carried out once a year by a firm of qualified accountants who are registered auditors.

  Certain small companies with a turnover of not more than £90,000 will be totally exempt from audit. Certain companies with a turnover of over £90,000 per annum but not more than £350,000 per annum, will be exempt from an audit but instead need an independent accountant's report. However, a third party, such as your bankers, may insist on an audit. Advice should be sought from your accountants as to whether you require an audit.
- A limited company must, each year, file with the Registrar of Companies a set of audited accounts, which include a directors' report, auditors' report, profit and loss account, balance sheet, cash flow and explanatory notes to the figures in the accounts. In addition it is necessary to file an annual return giving details of the directors, shareholders and certain other statutory information. All information on file at the Companies' Registry is open to inspection by the public.
- Registration of a limited company involves the filing of certain documents with the Registrar of Companies. While this is not unduly complicated, it is not a matter to be undertaken lightly and

involves a number of pitfalls. Professional advice should be sought. It is important to remember that the various documents, including the Memorandum and Articles of Association which give details of the company's constitution, its legal form, its business and its powers, have to be lodged with the Registrar of Companies before a company exists and can begin to trade.

Throughout the rest of this book the word 'company' refers to a limited liability company.

Unlimited company

A less common but sometimes useful entity is the unlimited company, which combines characteristics of both incorporated and unincorporated bodies in that, for taxation purposes, it is treated as a company, but the liability of the shareholders is unlimited as far as all creditors of the company are concerned.

There are certain businesses, regulated by professional bodies, which are required to trade as unlimited entities and, in some cases, an unlimited company is preferable to a partnership or sole proprietorship.

It is not unusual for a business to commence as a sole trader, become a partnership and ultimately incorporate as it grows.

Advantages and disadvantages

The decision as to which legal entity is appropriate to your particular circumstances is a complex matter and various advantages and disadvantages are listed below. In summary you should consider the following:

Sole trader/Partnership

Advantages
- Easy to start up.
- No legal formalities but partnerships should always have a partnership deed.
- Relative freedom from legislative control. No requirement to file audited accounts or information on public record concerning the business. Only accounts for VAT and PAYE required plus Inland Revenue tax return.
- No requirement to have an auditor.
- Taxed as self-employed which can have tax advantages in the first three years of trading.

- Advantageous rules on losses.
- Low National Insurance contributions. Self-employed pay Class 2 and Class 4 contributions:
  Class 2 – £5.75 per week (annual earnings exception limit £3,260)
  Class 4 – 7.30 per cent on profits between £6,640 and £22,880.
- More favourable tax treatment of deductible expenses for tax purposes. 'Wholly and exclusively ... for the purposes of the business' as opposed to 'Wholly, exclusively and necessarily in the performance of duties' for expenses of an employee of a company.
- Retirement relief provisions for capital gains tax are more flexible than those which apply to shareholdings in limited companies.
- Financial flexibility with regard to sharing profits.

Disadvantages
- Some suppliers will not deal with sole traders and partnerships owing to lack of statutory and 'financial control'.
- Unlimited liability. Unless there is a limited partnership an individual is liable for all losses of business; partners are jointly and severally liable.
- An individual could lose all his or her assets and therefore face bankruptcy.
- 'Closing' year's tax treatment when the business ceases – timing important.
- Profit taxed at personal rates, top rate being 40 per cent whether or not withdrawn from business.
- Need to make independent pension provision – less advantageous rules than for companies.
- Tax problems can arise on incorporating at a later stage.
- Raising finance can be difficult.
- Partnership can be difficult to run – direction a problem.
- No statutory protection of business name.

Limited company

Advantages
- Lower rate of tax on profits retained in business.
- Limited liability. Shareholders' liability limited to amount of share capital contributed.
- Favoured trading medium by suppliers as tightly controlled by statute.
- Directors not liable if they 'follow the rules' and act professionally.

- Ideal vehicle for expansion.
- Can give fixed and floating charges on company assets.
- Easier to pass the company down from generation to generation.
- Some business sectors require the 'kudos' of limited liability.
- Continuity of existence.
- Protection of company names.
- Tax efficient ways of getting shares into the hands of employees through employee share schemes.
- Vehicle for investment by Venture Capital Trust.
- Can split ownership and management (ie shareholders v directors).
- Company pension scheme can provide greater benefits than self-employed arrangements.

Disadvantages
- Limited liability could be negated in practice by director/shareholders having to give personal guarantees to third parties.
- Disclosure of information (for example, about the company through filing audited accounts, annual returns, Memorandum and Articles of Association).
- Tightly regulated through provisions in the Companies Acts, Insolvency Act 1986, Company Directors' Disqualification Act 1986.
- Heavy penalties under statute if rules 'not followed'. Also personal financial liability may be incurred.
- High set-up costs and annual running costs.
- High National Insurance contributions:
    Employer maximum 10.2 per cent
    Employee maximum 10 per cent.
- Directors paid under PAYE.
- Less beneficial treatment of deductible expenses and 'benefits in kind'.
- Less flexible profit-sharing arrangements.
- Statutory records to be kept.
- Stamp duty generally payable on transfers of shares.
- Double charge to capital gains tax
    - first charge on the company or gains made by selling its assets.
    - second charge on the shareholders realising their shares in the company.
- Directors cannot use business funds for personal use without an assessment to income tax as a benefit in kind arising.

Other factors linked to incorporation

Commercial considerations

Market-place image can be extremely important when starting a business because customers and suppliers must be inspired to trade with you confidently, and that means giving the impression that the organisation is well run and soundly based. For many people this is best suggested by adopting limited company status.

Like other images, this one is exaggerated; incorporation cannot ensure reliability or respectability. However, by becoming a company you show that you are willing to work within the controls and requirements of the Companies Act 1985.

Tax considerations

Commercial considerations should always outweigh tax considerations. However, if commercial considerations make little or no difference to the best form of business to adopt, consideration of the tax implications may help you to reach a decision.

A company is required to pay corporation tax and a sole trader or partnership income tax on profits earned. It is necessary to inform your local Inspector of Taxes of your existence and the following forms should be completed as appropriate:

CT41G	Inland Revenue Corporation Tax (for companies).
41G	Inland Revenue Income Tax (for sole traders and partnerships).
P222	PAYE: Particulars of Directors (for companies).
P223(1993)	Inland Revenue PAYE.
64–8	Notices of Assessment (authorising the Inland Revenue to send copies of the assessments to your professional advisers).

These forms are reproduced on pages 37–41.

Sole traders/Partnerships

Sole traders and partnerships are charged income tax at the rate applicable during the fiscal year (6 April to 5 April). The rates are as follows:

	1994/95			1995/96	
Tax band	Taxable income £	Rate	Tax band	Taxable income £	Rate
Lower	First 3,000	20%	Lower	First 3,200	20%
Basic	3,001 to 23,700	25%	Basic	3,201 to 24,300	25%
Higher	Over 23,700	40%	Higher	Over 24,300	40%

 **Inland Revenue**
Corporation Tax

Reference

The Secretary

Dear Sir/Madam,

I shall be grateful if you will supply the information requested overleaf and at the same time **forward a copy of the Company's Memorandum and Articles of Association for me to retain.**

May I remind you that -

● the company should

   - operate Pay As You Earn in respect of all remuneration paid (including fees, etc., paid or credited to directors)

   - deduct National Insurance Contributions

● the company is required to make returns to the Collector of Taxes

   - of all qualifying distributions and the Advance Corporation Tax payable in respect of them

   - of certain amounts of Franked Investment Income received, and

   - of all annual payments etc. and the income tax deducted from them

● the company should return this form in order to avoid the possibility of estimated assessments being issued.

You may like to take a photocopy of this form as a record of your reply.

Yours faithfully

District date stamp

HM Inspector of Taxes

CT41G

Printed in the UK for HMSO Dd.8183064 2/90 C1680 Gp.870 CCN 3832

**Inland Revenue
Income Tax**

Reference

District date stamp

I understand you may now be self employed (this includes subcontracting in the Construction Industry). If so please let me have the information asked for below and over the page as soon as possible.

If this is the first time you have been self employed, you may find booklet IR28 'Starting in Business' helpful. You can get this from any Tax Office. If you need any further help I shall be pleased to arrange an appointment for you to see me.

When you become self employed, you normally pay National Insurance Contributions (Class 2). Please get in touch with your local Social Security Office about this.

Enquiries about yourself and any business partners

Yourself

Your surname

Your first names

Your private address

Postcode

Tax Office to which last Income Tax Return made

Reference in that Office

National Insurance Number

Date of birth

Business partners

	Partner 1	Partner 2	Partner 3
Partner's surname			
Partner's first names			
Partner's private address			
	Postcode	Postcode	Postcode

If you have more than three business partners please give the names and addresses of any other partners on a separate sheet

41G

Please turn over

**Inland Revenue
PAYE**

Reference

District date stamp

Details of Directors

Please let me have the details asked for below. This will help me to give the directors the correct code numbers.

If the directors can tell you their last Tax Offices and reference numbers it may avoid separate enquiries to each director.

Surname, first name(s) and private address	National Insurance number	Last known Tax Office and reference
Postcode		
Postcode		
Postcode		
Postcode		
Postcode		

P222

Printed in the UK for HMSO Dd 8183067 3/90 C2500 Gp.870 CCN 3832

Inland Revenue

Employer information

Please give the information asked for on this form. If you have already given us some of the information we are sorry to ask you for it again, but completing this form will help us to make sure that, in future, we send you only the forms and information you really need.

General information

Trading name of the business

Business address and
phone number

Post code

Phone number

Brief description of business -
for example "grocery shop"

Name(s) of the Proprietor(s)
of the business

The date you began employing staff

If you are a limited company please enter the company's registration number.

Payroll information

Who will operate PAYE for your employees? *Tick **one** box only.*

You (or one of your employees)　　Your accountant (or financial adviser)　　A payroll agency

If you want information sent direct to the person who will be operating PAYE on your behalf or you are **not** going to operate PAYE from the address shown above, please enter the name and address of the person to contact below.

Name

Address

Post code

Phone number

P223 (1993)   *Please turn over*

Please read the notes on the back before completing this authority

To: H.M. Inspector of Taxes _____ **District**

Inspector's reference _____

| Reference |
| / |
| National Insurance number |

Name of person to be assessed _____

Until further notice, please send copies of any notices of assessment to income tax, Class 4 NIC, corporation tax and capital gains tax, and any explanatory forms which accompany those notices, to

Agent's name _____

Full address _____

_____

_____ Postcode _____

Agent's reference _____

I withdraw any earlier request that copies of notices of assessment should be sent to any other agent.

* I would like this authority to be applied to all my income or gains currently subject to assessment.

Signature _____ Date _____ 19 ___
* delete as appropriate

For official use   Initials   Date

Taxpayer's record noted _____ _____

133U/133U-1/133P-1 or CT133 noted _____ _____

Form(s) 64-6 issued _____ _____

Form 670 issued where agent's code not known _____ _____
                      companies only

Form CZ1 or CZ4 issued companies only _____ _____

64-8

There may also be a liability to Class 2 and Class 4 National Insurance contributions depending on the level of profit in each fiscal year. Class 2 contributions are at a weekly stamp rate of £5.75. Class 4 contributions are levied at 7.3 per cent on profits between £6640 and £22,880 (maximum; 1994–5 rates). Income tax and Class 4 National Insurance contributions are due in two instalments on 1 January and 1 July.

Companies

Companies are charged corporation tax at the rate applicable during the financial year, which for tax purposes runs from 1 April to 31 March. Where a company's year end is not 31 March, the profits for the year are apportioned and the appropriate rate charged.

The corporation tax rates applicable for the years 1993–1996 are:

Accounts year end	Rate	Small companies' profits below £	Rate	Normal rate profits over £
31 March 1993 & 1994	25%	250,000	33%	1,250,000
31 March 1995 & 1996	25%	300,000	33%	1,500,000

The rates for profits falling between the small companies and normal rates are such as to ensure that the tax charge rises progressively and that the overall tax paid is between the small and normal company rates.

Corporation tax Pay and File was brought into effect for accounting periods ending after 30 September 1993. A company is required to make an estimate of its own liability to corporation tax and pay that liability by the normal due date, nine months after the end of the accounting period, without an assessment being raised.

The company is required to send its completed tax return, accounts and tax computation to the Inspector by the filing date, which is 12 months after the end of its accounting period. Penalties will be charged if it does not.

Once the company agrees its liability with the Inspector, there will be a settlement of any balance due or overpaid. Interest will be charged or paid from the normal due date on the balance.

Remuneration

Sole traders/Partnerships

In this situation the owner of the business or the partner is treated as a self-employed individual. Drawings can be made from the business during the course of the year without paying tax, but the owner is liable to pay tax on all profits whether drawn out of the business or not.

Shareholders/Proprietors
In a limited company the shareholders may also be directors of the company. For tax purposes they are treated as employees of the company and all remuneration paid to them must be subject to tax under the PAYE system.

Personal considerations
The degree of risk which an individual runs depends partly on the form of business structure adopted. Theoretically, a sole trader takes the greater risk in that he or she must meet the liabilities of the business out of his or her own funds if necessary. The members of a partnership are in a similar position, although they may have a wider asset base. Shareholders in a limited company know that the most they can lose is the money they paid for their shares, unless personal guarantees have been made to a bank or another third party.

Each person's attitude to risk depends upon personal opinions and circumstances. There are many other factors which can only be weighed by the individual, such as the following:

- Do I have sufficient business acumen to run a business by myself, or would it be wiser to collaborate with other people who have complementary skills?
- Am I prepared to have the operation of the business governed by the restrictions of company law?
- Am I prepared to pay incorporation and audit costs?
- Do I have long-term plans for the business and the financing of it, or do I envisage a short-term venture to take advantage of temporary market opportunities?
- A further consideration now stems from the provisions of the Insolvency Act 1986 in respect of the disqualification and personal liability of directors, and the next section is devoted to the responsibilities of directors in general and to their potential liabilities in particular.

Duties of directors

Anyone who sets out in business and forms a company will find him or herself having to take on the role and responsibilities of a director. This role may be described as the overall direction, management and operation of the company.

To satisfy the law, a private company must have at least one director. There must also be a company secretary, and a sole director cannot also be the company secretary.

The first directors of a company are usually appointed by the subscribers to the company's Memorandum and Articles of Association, the documents which give details of the company's constitution, legal form, its business and its powers.

Thereafter, the directors normally have the power, at any time, to appoint a person to fill a vacancy caused by the sudden departure of a director from the board, or to appoint an additional director. A company may remove a director and appoint another person in his or her place.

The company's Articles of Association may disqualify a director from acting as such in certain circumstances, or may require that his or her office be vacated. Such circumstances include:

- if a director becomes bankrupt or of unsound mind;
- if he or she is convicted of an offence in connection with the promotion, formation or management of the company, or of any fraud;
- if, by notice in writing, he or she resigns the office of director; or
- if he or she is absent from board meetings for more than six months without the other directors' permission.

Conduct of directors

The general principles of current law governing the accountability of directors may be dealt with under two headings: good faith, and skill and care.

Good faith

A director must observe the utmost good faith towards the company in any transaction with it or on its behalf. As an agent and officer of the company, the director must exercise the powers vested in him or her in the interests of the company as a whole, having regard to the interests of the company's employees as well as those of its shareholders. Since the director is in a position of trust, he or she must disregard private interests where there might be a conflict.

The director must act honestly and with diligence in exercising the powers of office, and where any power is exercised it must be for the purpose for which it was intended. A director may not, therefore, make a personal profit from information or opportunities arising from his or her position as director; any such profit must be accounted for to the company.

Skill and care

In the case of an executive director, usually appointed for some expertise, and under a contract of service, it is implied in such a contract that the person will exercise reasonable skill and care which can be expected of someone in his or her position.

In the case of a non-executive director without relevant qualifications or experience in business, the skill and care expected is subjective; that is, the director must do his or her best.

For a director having particular qualifications and/or experience in business the standard is objective: he or she is bound to exercise such skill and care as may be expected from a person of such professional skill or experience.

Under the Insolvency Act 1986, a court can disqualify a director from office for a minimum period of two years where he or she is or has been a director of a company that has become insolvent, and where his or her conduct as a director of that company makes him or her unfit to be involved in the management of any company. The Act applies equally if the director has been incompetent or dishonest. Moreover, the provisions apply where a company has gone into insolvent liquidation and he or she was a director of the company in the 24 months preceding the liquidation, as there is an assumed duty to persuade colleagues on the board of the error of their ways, and to insist that they take competent and timely advice.

In addition, if, at some time before the winding-up of a company, a director knew or ought to have concluded that there was no reasonable prospect of that company avoiding insolvent liquidation, a court, on application by the liquidator, may ask the director to contribute to that company's assets as the court thinks proper.

Thus, the Insolvency Act has introduced responsibilities which any individual considering incorporation would be foolish to overlook.

Co-operatives

Another possibility in starting a business would be to form a co-operative with your fellow workers. In such an organisation the running of the business is controlled by its workforce, ie they make the decisions on who should manage the business, safeguard assets and what its aims are to be.

It is still necessary to establish a legal entity. This can take the form of a partnership, limited company or registration as a co-operative society.

Franchising

A franchise system operates on the basis that an entrepreneur (known as the franchisor) will have developed a particular business (eg a print shop providing photocopying facilities, printing, stationery etc, or a hamburger restaurant) and wishes to expand into other locations by granting a franchise to another party (the franchisee) to operate a similar business. The franchisor will make sure that the franchisee is a suitable person to run the business, and it is equally important for the franchisee to make full and careful investigation of how successful the particular franchise is and to talk to existing franchisees. Once the parties agree, the franchisee will normally make an initial payment to the franchisor and in return will receive help and advice in setting up the business. The franchisee will have to deal with all the matters in relation to raising finance, preparing a business plan and establishing a legal entity as mentioned before. The franchisee will continue to make payments to the franchisor, usually based on levels of turnover or profit.

The main advantages of a franchise are that a lot of the initial problems of setting up a business will be relieved by the help and experience of the franchisor and that you are working with an established business. The element of risk in setting up your business is therefore reduced.

The main disadvantage is that, while it is your own business, there will be a significant level of control by, and you will be paying a proportion of your income to, the franchisor. You may wish to take greater risks in establishing your own business in the hope of higher rewards.

Before entering into any franchising agreement it is essential that you obtain professional advice from your accountant or solicitor.

5

Setting Up the Business

Introduction

This chapter covers in detail the various matters which will need consideration, and in many instances action, before your trading entity can make the first product, sell the first item or supply the first service.

These matters are as follows:

- bank accounts must be opened;
- trading premises must be found;
- trading terms must be set;
- relevant authorities must be informed;
- if employees are recruited, a PAYE scheme must be set up;
- application for VAT registration must be made;
- letterheads, invoices and stationery must be printed, and nameplates obtained; and
- insurance cover must be obtained.

Bank accounts and cheque signatories

Before trading commences, it will be necessary to open a current account with a bank, and possibly also a deposit account. The bank will require completion of a mandate and copies of the Articles of Association and Certificate of Incorporation in the case of a company.

In doing this you will need to decide who the cheque signatories will be, and determine their level of authority. The bank should then be informed of these details in writing, and given instructions as to the provision of pre-printed cheque books and paying-in books, how frequently you will require bank statements – at least monthly, but possibly more often than that – and details of standing orders, direct debits and credit transfers required.

Very frequently, at the start-up of a new business, overdraft and/or loan facilities are required and you will have prepared a business plan as described in Chapter 2. In the case of an unincorporated business, the bank may demand that their loan or overdraft is secured on property belonging to the proprietor, which may or may not be part of the assets of the business. In the case of companies, banks frequently require personal guarantees from the directors and a charge over the company's assets (known as a debenture). Professional advice should be sought from your accountant or solicitor before completing the documentation required by the bank.

The bank will also wish to know how your business is progressing and to make comparisons against your original budgets and cash flows. You will need to agree the frequency with which you supply the bank manager with copies of your management accounts and other information as described in Chapter 8.

Where are you going to trade from?

The acquisition of property is a complex process and you need to give yourself plenty of time and plan well in advance of commencing business. Many businesses commence trading from home and, while this will achieve cost savings initially, it is likely that you will quickly outgrow the space available. Professional advice is essential but before taking such advice you should consider the following:

Initial considerations

- The type of building may be important. Many older buildings have awkward shapes which may not be suitable to your business and cause inefficiencies. A small light industrial unit or a new warehouse may be more suitable and give you the scope to design the interior to your particular needs.
- Check that the building can be used for both office and factory purposes. Many buildings, particularly older ones, are used for purposes not permitted by the local authority.
- The building should be large enough for your present and anticipated near future requirements.
- Ensure that the utilities (gas, electricity etc) you require are available and in sufficient quantity for your needs.
- Consider parking and loading areas around your premises.
- What are the security arrangements for the site? Will you have to install a sophisticated security system yourself?

- What other items are there specific to your particular business (waste disposal, ventilation etc)?

Where do you want to be?
The location of your premises will often be essential to the success of your business and you need to think about the following questions:

- Should it be a retail location?
- What are the local transport facilities and proximity to trunk routes?
- How close are you to suppliers/customers?
- Are the skills that you need available in the area?
- Are there any town planning requirements/restrictions?
- Where is your competition?
- What grants are available?
- Any personal reason (where you live, family commitments, schools etc)?

What sort of premises do you need?
The following matters should be considered:

- The amount of space required (splitting between office, factory, warehouse).
- The type of building – is a prominent or prestigious building necessary (and can you afford it)?

What type of building do you require?
There are both advantages and disadvantages in new and existing buildings, some of which are set out below for consideration:

- A new building will have lower repair and maintenance costs, at least for the first five to ten years.
- A new building will have better thermal insulation, thus reducing heating bills, and will have been designed to comply with current health and safety and fire regulations, which may be expensive to update in an older building.
- A new building can be designed to your own requirements, and to allow for future expansion, but it may be difficult and expensive to make alterations to an existing building.
- A new building may look cleaner and more impressive and this may be important if you expect your customers to come to you.
- There is more choice of older buildings available on the market at any time, and you will probably be able to move in more quickly than if a building is designed and built to your specific requirements.

- An existing building will probably be cheaper to rent or buy.
- An older building will generally not hold its value as an investment as well as a new building, particularly if the location is poor.
- While it may be cheaper to acquire or lease an older property the cost of conversion may ultimately mean higher costs than acquiring a purpose-built factory. It is essential that you list the pros and cons and determine which is the most cost efficient in the long term.

Are you going to buy or lease?

You will need to consider whether you will purchase the property outright from the previous owner (freehold) or lease over a period of time from the owner (leasehold).

In general terms, freehold is preferable to leasehold property as you will have the benefit of capital appreciation and, as long as you remain within the law, be able to do what you like with it. If you outgrow your premises, it should be easier to dispose of a freehold rather than a leasehold property.

However, on a practical note, most new businesses cannot afford to purchase a building outright and find both interest and capital repayments on the funds borrowed to buy the property. Therefore, the first major commitment of a company is often the acquisition of leasehold premises.

Leases are invariably lengthy and complex legal documents requiring the expert consideration of your solicitor. When considering a lease you need to bear in mind the following:

- If the lease is a new one, the company will remain responsible for it for its entire duration, even if management later assign or sublet the property. Landlords can bring actions for recovery of outstanding rents unpaid by the present tenant against the previous tenant unless the previous tenant was specifically released from all covenants under the lease.
- The landlord may require personal guarantees from the directors of a company.
- You may wish to assign the lease or sublet the premises. Are there any restrictions in the lease?
- What is the period of the rent review (normally, three, five or seven years)?
- If you carry out improvements to the premises, will these be reflected in your next rent review?
- What is the length of the lease and any break points (options to terminate by one party or the other)?
- Are there any restrictions on the use of the premises?
- What is your liability to dilapidations?

Who can you go to for help?

Professionals: chartered surveyors and estate agents
Advice should be sought from friends and colleagues with a personal knowledge of the professional firms in your area before you select one to find a property for you. You should agree terms in advance, and brief the agent in detail as to your requirements and price range. He or she will then negotiate the best deal possible on your behalf. These professional firms are also particularly qualified to act for you in planning matters, and in valuations if required for a mortgage application.

Local and national newspapers
Studying the industrial and commercial property advertisements in the press will give you a good idea of availability and price.

Other support
The range of support, both financial and advisory, is extensive. Appendix 9 contains a list of contact addresses and telephone numbers where support and advice is available to anyone starting up in business. These contacts will usually produce literature which can assist you in deciding whether they can be of assistance to you.

Have you thought of the other costs?
Your budget should also include the add-on costs of acquiring premises:

- Removals to the premises if applicable.
- Fitting out the various areas for the purposes for which they will be used, and arranging for gas, electricity and water to be laid on. You may also need to arrange for refuse collection and purchase the appropriate containers.
- Furniture and equipment for the office which may include desks, chairs, filing cabinets, shelves, calculators, typewriters, word processors, a computer system, photocopiers, communications equipment ranging from telephone and telex to a facsimile machine and computer modems, vending machines and/or tea- and coffee-making facilities, perhaps a fridge, first aid equipment, fire extinguishers etc.
- Stationery will need to be printed ready for you to use as soon as you move to new premises.
- Health and safety regulations. The rules and regulations are fairly complex. Advice on health and safety matters is given by Inspectors, and there is an extensive amount of technical material published by

the Health and Safety Executive. A visit from the Health and Safety Officer can result in an unprepared company incurring additional expenditure.

● Fire regulations are strict and you should arrange for an inspection by a fire officer so that any costs of complying with the regulations can be allowed for in your budget.

Trading terms

Before you start you should set your terms of trade in relation to your sales. To a large extent these will probably be dictated by those of your competitors. Matters which you should consider are:

● responsibility for shipment and related costs;
● point at which title transfers to the buyer;
● insurance for goods in transit;
● terms of credit and discounts;
● method of payment;
● appointment of agents, if appropriate;
● period during which you will accept returned goods;
● period for which quotations will be held;
● arrangements for the cancellation of orders.

Before printing these, your solicitor should be asked to review your trading terms to ensure that they give you adequate protection and that they are legally enforceable.

Finally, these conditions must form part of the 'offer for sale' that you are making to your customers, and therefore it is essential that they are brought to the customers' attention. If they are printed on the back of quotations, order forms etc, attention should be drawn to them on the front of the form. They should also be on display at your premises, and printed in catalogues and price lists.

Pay As You Earn (PAYE)

Deduction of income tax and National Insurance contributions (NIC) under the PAYE system is obligatory for all organisations that have employees, including directors. Whether or not an individual is an employee in a particular situation is a question of fact depending on the terms under which he or she works. It is important for this to be clarified before an individual is taken on.

The following principal factors should be taken into account:

- the degree of control exercised over the individual's work;
- whether services are performed wholly or mainly for one business;
- where the duties are carried out;
- terms of pay, holiday time, pension arrangements and other benefits;
- whether the work has to be performed personally, or whether a substitute may be supplied;
- provision of own items of equipment;
- the financial risk and responsibility undertaken by the individual.

The Inland Revenue have issued leaflet IR56, entitled 'Tax: Employed or Self-employed' which sets out the guidelines of employment status; if doubt exists it should be clarified, and the Revenue have indicated that they expect to be consulted on difficult or uncertain cases. Obtaining prior Revenue agreement will avoid having to make a settlement later of liabilities to tax or National Insurance which the employer failed to deduct from the remuneration of a person who is held to be an employee rather than self-employed.

Having ascertained that you will need to operate PAYE, it is necessary to notify the Revenue office covering your geographical area. The telephone number of the nearest PAYE enquiry office is listed in the telephone directory; from them the name of the Revenue office can be obtained.

The relevant forms which need to be submitted to the Inland Revenue were described in the previous chapter.

Upon registration, the Inland Revenue will send you:

- a PAYE reference number;
- Form P8 'How to operate the PAYE system' (introduction for employers to tax tables, completion of deductions working sheets, new and leaving employees etc);
- Employers' Guides to PAYE, National Insurance, Statutory Sick Pay (SSP) and Statutory Maternity Pay (SMP);
- supplies of the following forms:
  - P11 Deductions working sheet
  - P15 Coding claim form for completion by new employee
  - P45 Details of employee leaving
  - P46 Notification to the Revenue where a new employee does not produce parts 2 and 3 of Form P45
  - P47 Application for authority to refund tax to new employee in excess of £200.

More information is given in Appendix 5.

In order to calculate the amount of tax and National Insurance payable by an employee, the Inland Revenue will supply you with sets of tables. By reference to 'Free Pay Tables' and an employee's tax code, you will be able to calculate the amount of salary which is not subject to tax at the end of the payment period. The difference between this and the gross salary is the employee's 'taxable pay'. The tax can then be calculated by reference to the 'Taxable Pay Tables'. The employer's and employee's National Insurance contributions are calculated by reference to the employee's gross pay in conjunction with the 'National Insurance Tables'.

Employers are also required to pay Statutory Sick Pay (SSP) to their employees who are off work for four or more days as a result of illness, accident or injury. The amount of SSP payable is laid down, and depends on the employee's average earnings for the preceding eight-week period. Total SSP payable (plus a percentage to compensate the employer for the employer's NIC) is deducted from the total National Insurance contributions payable to the Inland Revenue. The 'Employer's Guide to Statutory Sick Pay' gives detailed guidance on the operation of SSP.

Statutory Maternity Pay (SMP) works like SSP in that it is paid to the employee in the same way that she would be paid her wages. SMP paid (plus compensation for employer's NIC) is then deducted from the National Insurance contributions payable to the Collector of Taxes. The 'Employer's Guide to Statutory Maternity Pay' sets out all the rules governing the administration of SMP.

The tax and National Insurance due (after deduction of any SSP and SMP paid) should be paid over to the Inland Revenue by the 19th of the month following that in which the salary is paid.

At the end of each year (5 April) the employer will be sent forms for completion summarising each employee's pay, deductions and SSP/SMP paid for the year (P14) and the employer's annual statement (P35), a summary form on which the employees are listed, with their total deductions and SSP/SMP for the year. These amounts are totalled and added to the amounts accounted for by the employer to the Inland Revenue.

In addition to deducting tax and National Insurance contributions during the year, an employer will have to complete returns at the end of the year which give details of expenses paid or reimbursed to employees during the year and also benefits provided.

Form P9D is used for employees earning less than £8500 per annum; Form P11D relates to employees earning more than this amount and all directors regardless of levels of remuneration.

In deciding whether the £8500 limit has been reached, it is necessary to include not only salary or wages but also the value of taxable benefits and reimbursed expenses before any claim is made for business use.

These forms will be issued to employers at the end of the tax year together with details regarding their completion. The forms are wide-ranging and employers should ensure that their records of employee expenses and benefits are sufficient to enable them to be completed. The non-completion or incorrect completion of these forms is an area which the Inland Revenue frequently investigate and which can lead to substantial tax liabilities and penalties if they are not sent to the Inland Revenue by the due date.

Value Added Tax (VAT)

A trader is required to register for VAT purposes if annual taxable turnover is expected to exceed £46,000 per annum. A 'taxable person' (a person or company who is registered or required to be registered under the VAT legislation) is required to account for VAT on supplies made (output tax) but is entitled to claim credit for VAT suffered or paid by him or her on goods or services supplied to him or her (input tax). If input tax exceeds output tax, a taxable person may claim a refund of the excess. Taxable persons therefore act as collecting agents for the tax. VAT is collected by HM Customs and Excise.

You can also apply for voluntary registration to reclaim net input tax. This can be beneficial in the early days of a business to enable you to reclaim VAT on the purchase of capital equipment and stock. Once registered for VAT a business will be expected to remain so for two years before de-registration can be considered.

Registration is obtained by completing Form VAT1 (reproduced on pages 57–59) with Form VAT 2 for a partnership (page 60), which can be obtained from your local VAT office (listed in the telephone directory) and returning it to them. They also have available numerous free publications explaining the VAT legislation and how it applies to different trades. In particular, the booklet 'Should I be registered for VAT?' will be of use to new businesses. There are various options available when determining how to account for the tax. It is advisable to consult your accountant as to the most appropriate method for your business.

There are currently three rates of tax:

- Standard rate – 17½ per cent
- Zero rate – 0 per cent
- Intermediate rate – 8 per cent (currently fuel only).

The majority of businesses will charge VAT at the rate of 17½ per cent but some businesses (eg farms, publishers) make predominantly zero-rated supplies. Consequently, their input tax frequently exceeds their output tax. Businesses of this nature regularly find repayments of tax due to them from Customs and Excise.

Certain supplies are exempt from VAT. These include supplies made by financial institutions, insurance brokers and certain educational organisations. Businesses making wholly exempt supplies cannot register for VAT. Those making some exempt and some taxable supplies may be able to register for VAT. However, businesses in this situation may find that they are unable to reclaim all the input tax which they incur on expenses.

You should note particularly that VAT in relation to the construction industry and transactions in land and property is complex. In addition, the harmonisation of British and European legislation makes it advisable to seek professional guidance in order to maximise planning opportunities and minimise the risk of incurring penalties.

If a potential 'taxable person', who is liable to register because he or she has exceeded the turnover limits, fails to notify Customs and Excise at the correct time, his or her registration may be backdated and the 'taxable person' may have to account for tax on turnover since that date even though that person may not have charged VAT to customers. Customs and Excise may also levy a non-mitigable penalty.

Once registered, VAT returns (Form VAT 100) are usually made quarterly, although you can apply for a monthly return period if repayments are anticipated. It will reduce the amount of accounting if you ensure that the quarterly VAT return coincides with your year end. The VAT return, together with any tax due, must be submitted within one month of the end of the period to which it relates. Heavy penalties/ interest are imposed for late returns, late payment or incorrect returns.

HM Customs and Excise are also empowered to carry out 'VAT audits' to ensure that a trader is accounting for VAT correctly; full-scale investigations can be undertaken by Customs and Excise if they believe that the VAT regulations are being abused.

Letterheads, invoices and nameplates

The design of your logo and stationery can be an important part of your marketing strategy, as letters, invoices, mail shots and statements are all forms of public relations.

Company

The business letters and order forms of a company must clearly show the

H M Customs
and Excise

VALUE ADDED TAX

Application for Registration

Issuing Office

For Official use	
Issue code.	*19404*
Date of receipt	

VAT 1 CD 2810/ND(10/93)   F 3733 (JAN 94)

9. Please read NOTE 9 in the leaflet before you answer this question

Have you made any TAXABLE SUPPLIES yet?

YES ☐   I MADE my first supply on ☐☐☐   *Go to 10*

NO ☐   But I INTEND TO start on ☐☐☐

You **must** enclose EVIDENCE to support your application.   *Go to 11*

10. Has the VALUE of your business's TAXABLE SUPPLIES in the last 12 months OR LESS exceeded the registration limit? (see note 10)

YES ☐ *Go to 12*   NO ☐ *Go to 11*

11. Will the TOTAL value of TAXABLE SUPPLIES which you will make in the NEXT 30 DAYS exceed the registration limit?

YES ☐ *Go to 12*   NO ☐ *Go to 13*

12. If the answer to EITHER QUESTION 10 or 11 is YES from what date MUST you be REGISTERED for VAT?

(see note 12 - this is VERY IMPORTANT)

I am REQUIRED to be registered from ☐☐☐

But I would LIKE TO BE registered from this earlier date ☐☐☐   *Go to 14*

13. I am NOT REQUIRED to be registered but I WISH TO BE registered from ☐☐☐   *Go to 14*

14. Please enter the ESTIMATED VALUE of TAXABLE SUPPLIES you expect to make in the next 12 months ☐

15. What VALUE of GOODS are you likely to sell to or buy from other EC Countries in the next 12 months? (Leave blank if NIL)   SELL £ ☐   BUY £ ☐

16. Do you wish to request EXEMPTION from registration because all your supplies are ZERO RATED?

YES ☐ and my ZERO RATED supplies amount to £ ☐ in the next 12 months

NO ☐

17. Do you expect to be ENTITLED to REGULAR REPAYMENTS of VAT? (Tick one box)   YES ☐   NO ☐

18. Are there any other VAT REGISTRATIONS in which you are involved (see note 18 if in doubt)?

YES ☐ If YES please enter the registration numbers in the boxes provided.   ☐☐☐   (Please continue on a separate sheet if necessary)

NO ☐   ☐☐☐

☐☐☐

19. YOU MUST COMPLETE THE FOLLOWING DECLARATION IN FULL (see note 19)

I .... (enter your full name in BLOCK LETTERS)
DECLARE that the information entered on this form and contained in any accompanying documents is true and complete.

Signature .... Date ....

Tick ONE box   Proprietor ☐   Director ☐   Trustee ☐

Partner ☐   Company Secretary ☐   Authorised Official ☐

CD 2810/ND(10/93)

Local office code
and registration
number

Name

E D M Y
D
R

Stagger   Status

Trade name

Trade classification   Taxable Turnover

Repl. Vol. Oversize name address Comp. user Group Div Intg Overseas   Intg. EC   Value of Sales from EC   Value of Purchases to EC

Registration	Obligatory/Voluntary	Exemption	Intending	Transfer of Regn No.
Approved - Initial/date				
Refused - Initial/date				
Form issued - initial/date	VAT 9/ Other	VAT 8	Letter	Approval letter

Application For VAT Registration

You should read the notes in the registration leaflet "Should I be Registered for VAT?" which will help you to answer these questions. Failure to answer questions correctly may result in a delay in your registration number being advised to you.
Please write clearly in black ink.
VAT 1 CD 2812GND(10/92)   **Do not detach**

1. Enter your FULL NAME. Write in BLOCK LETTERS and leave a space between words

2. Enter your TRADING NAME if it is different from the name entered at 1

3. Enter the address of your PRINCIPAL PLACE OF BUSINESS

Phone No.

Postcode

4. Describe your main BUSINESS ACTIVITY IN FULL please (see note 4)

5. Who is the BUSINESS OWNED by ? (see note 5 and tick ONE BOX only)

Sole Proprietor

or Partnership   if partnership please ensure you ALSO complete form VAT 2

or Limited Company   Please enter details from Company Incorporation Certificate below.

Certificate Number   Date of certificate

or Other   Please give details

6. Was your BUSINESS TRANSFERRED to you or your company as a GOING CONCERN?

YES   NO   if YES, enter the date of transfer   and also

Enter the PREVIOUS OWNER'S name

and VAT REGISTRATION NUMBER

Do you want to RETAIN the VAT NUMBER of the previous owner?   YES   NO   (see note 6)

If you tick YES then both you and the previous owner MUST also complete form VAT 68

7. Enter EITHER your BANK SORT CODE   and ACCOUNT NUMBER   or your GIROBANK ACCOUNT NUMBER

8. Do you use a COMPUTER FOR ACCOUNTING? (see note 8 and tick one box only)   YES   NO

CD 2812GND(10/92)

VALUE ADDED TAX
Partnership Details

HM Customs and Excise

Each partner should complete one of the sections below.

Please start at the beginning of each line and leave a space between words.

Please use BLOCK CAPITALS and write clearly in ink.

Registration No. (where known)

Partner details

1

Full name

Home Address

Home Telephone

Signature _____ Date _____ Postcode

Partner details

2

Full name

Home Address

Home Telephone

Signature _____ Date _____ Postcode

Partner details

3

Full name

Home Address

Home Telephone

Signature _____ Date _____ Postcode

Partner details

4

Full name

Home Address

Home Telephone

Signature _____ Date _____ Postcode

VAT 2

please continue overleaf ———▶

Value Added Tax Return
For the period
to

HM Customs
and Excise

For Official Use

Registration number   Period

You could be liable to a financial penalty if your completed return and all the VAT payable are not received by the due date.

Due date:

For official use D O R only

Before you fill in this form please read the notes on the back and the VAT leaflet *"Filling in your VAT return"*. Fill in all boxes clearly in ink, and write 'none' where necessary. Don't put a dash or leave any box blank. If there are no pence write "00" in the pence column. Do not enter more than one amount in any box.

For official use			£	p
	VAT due in this period on sales and other outputs	**1**		
	VAT due in this period on acquisitions from other EC Member States	**2**		
	Total VAT due (the sum of boxes 1 and 2)	**3**		
	VAT reclaimed in this period on purchases and other inputs (including acquisitions from the EC)	**4**		
	Net VAT to be paid to Customs or reclaimed by you (Difference between boxes 3 and 4)	**5**		
	Total value of sales and all other outputs excluding any VAT. Include your box 8 figure	**6**		00
	Total value of purchases and all other inputs excluding any VAT. Include your box 9 figure	**7**		00
	Total value of all supplies of goods and related services, excluding any VAT, to other EC Member States	**8**		00
	Total value of all acquisitions of goods and related services, excluding any VAT, from other EC Member States	**9**		00
	Retail schemes. If you have used any of the schemes in the period covered by this return, enter the relevant letter(s) in this box.			

DECLARATION: You, or someone on your behalf, must sign below.

If you are enclosing a payment please tick this box.

I, ...declare that the
(Full name of signatory in BLOCK LETTERS)

information given above is true and complete.

Signature ....Date ....19..............
A false declaration can result in prosecution.

VAT 100

country of registration and number under which it is registered, the address of the registered office and the address of the place of business if it is different from the registered office. It is not essential to list the names of the directors of the company, but if they are to be specified, they must all be named. If directors are named, the nationality must be noted of those who are not EU nationals.

The name of the company must also be shown on its notices, official publications, bills of exchange, promissory notes, endorsements, cheques and orders for money or goods, invoices, receipts and letters of credit. A nameplate must also appear outside each office (including the registered office) or place of business. Invoices must state the VAT registration number.

The table on page 63 sets out the legal requirements.

Partnership

All business letters, written orders for goods or services, invoices, receipts and written demands must either clearly state the name of each partner and the address within Great Britain where any documents may be served upon him or her, or state where a list of partners may be inspected. A notice containing the names and addresses of all the partners must be prominently displayed in any place where the partnership business is carried on. Invoices must state the VAT registration number.

Sole trader

A sole trader may carry on business under a name other than his own. It is not necessary to register the business name, although it must be shown on all business documentation, together with the address from which business is conducted. A sole trader is not obliged to put up a nameplate, but it may be advantageous to do so to inform passers-by of your existence. Invoices must state the VAT registration number.

Insurances

Before starting trading you should review the insurance cover that you require with an insurance broker.

Basically, there are two categories of cover:

Compulsory cover

A business is required to effect third-party insurance as follows:

- employer's liability – personal injury or damage to personal property of employees;
- motor insurance for all vehicles.

Letterheads, invoices and nameplates

Information	Letters	Orders	Invoices	Cheques	Official publications and forms	Premises
Name of company	Yes	Yes	Yes	Yes	Yes	Yes
Country of registration	Yes	Yes				Yes
Address of registered office	Yes	Yes				
Company number	Yes	Yes				
VAT number			Yes			
Forename or initials and surname (and nationality of non-EU directors) of ALL or NONE of the directors	Yes	Yes				

Voluntary cover

It is advisable to seek advice and to obtain quotations on the following additional insurances:

- public liability – personal injury or damage to personal property of the public;
- property damage – fire and theft, storm and flood water damage;
- product liability – indemnity against a product which has been manufactured, treated or repaired and causes injury or damage to a third party;
- business interruption – consequential loss of profits resulting from fire, theft etc;
- computer damage;
- bad debt cover;
- goods in transit.

Other insurances

Specialist insurances, dependent upon the business operated, for instance professional indemnity cover, should be considered.

Key man insurance should also be taken out if the business is dependent for its future on certain individuals. It may also be appropriate for the directors/proprietors to take out life assurance policies on each other.

You should note that all contracts of insurance are contracts of the utmost good faith, and therefore when completing proposal forms full disclosure must be made. Failure to observe this could render an insurance contract invalid.

6
Employing People

Good employees are valuable assets and therefore as much care and attention should be given to recruitment as to any other aspect of the business. Getting recruitment wrong can be a costly exercise, not only in terms of the time and money invested in a new employee, but also the lost performance, disruption to the business and the 'knock-on' demotivating effect on other employees. It is essential, therefore, to get recruitment right.

The employment of people carries heavy responsibilities and should not be undertaken lightly. There is extensive legislation relating to employment in general and especially to the health and safety of people at work.

Although the term 'company' has been used throughout this chapter, the regulations apply to all businesses, whatever their legal entity.

Contracts of employment

A contract of employment exists as soon as an employee proves his or her acceptance of an employer's terms and conditions of employment by starting work, and both employer and employee are bound by the terms offered and agreed.

Under the Trade Union Reform and Employment Rights Act 1993 (TURERA 93) within two months of an employee starting work, the employer must give the employee a principal statement of terms and conditions of employment ('the principal statement') in writing which must contain certain particulars regarding terms and conditions of employment and statement detailing disciplinary and grievance procedures.

Such principal statement may be given to an employee in addition to a formal contract of employment, or may be contained within such a contract.

A draft specimen statement of terms and conditions of employment is included in Appendix 6. This complies with the minimum legal requirement, but you should consult with your solicitor to tailor the statement to your particular needs.

Employment rights

TURERA 93 also provides certain statutory rights for the employees. Some are dependent upon the employee completing a period of continuous service with the company, but a number of rights arise as soon as employment commences.

Details of these rights are given in Appendix 7.

Health and safety

Ultimate responsibility for the health and safety of a company's employees, and those affected by the company's activities, rests with the employer.

Health and safety at work is primarily regulated by safety legislation. The rules and regulations are becoming increasingly complex, particularly with the implementation of new European directives and amendments to existing laws.

The Health and Safety Executive publish an extensive amount of technical material and advice is readily available from your local Health Inspector.

Wages, tax and National Insurance

Usually it is up to the company to set the rate of pay for the job, although it may be necessary to take account of whether national or local union agreements exist in the industry. Wages Orders still protect the rights of employees who were covered by them when Wages Councils were abolished in 1993. The amount of remuneration and the manner in which it is paid are agreed between the employer and the employee. Employees are entitled to receive an itemised statement, showing gross pay, deductions and the amount of net pay.

Details of the PAYE system are given in Chapter 5 and Appendix 5.

Disciplinary rules and procedures

It is important that a company has clear and well-understood disciplinary rules and procedures. Employees should have a copy of these. By following these rules consistently and fairly when any disciplinary problem arises, a company will minimise the risk of a finding of unfair dismissal.

A code of practice on disciplinary procedures is available from the local Arbitration and Conciliation Advisory Service (ACAS) offices.

The law in relation to disciplinary procedures is extremely complex and you are advised to consult your solicitor or ACAS.

7

Marketing the Product or Service

Market research

Whatever their talents, all people have one thing in common when they start up a new business – no customers, no business. Many people setting up in business have a vague idea that there are lots of people out there who need them. This is a very pleasant thought and good for the ego, but it will not pay the costs of setting up and running a business and it will not convince your bank manager to lend you money. To build a business you have to persuade people either to switch their custom from another supplier or to spend their money in a different way. In either case you have to persuade them to write cheques to you rather than to somebody else.

When you are starting a business, the way to understand better whether customers really exist for your particular product or service is to ask a number of questions. Examples include:

- How many potential customers are there?
- How many real customers are there?
- Who are they?
- When is the buying done?
- What kind of products or services do they want to buy?
- Why do they want the product or service?
- Where do they get it at present?
- How much do they pay at the moment?
- How much will they pay for my product?
- What deficiencies are there in the products or services which they buy at the moment?
- When do customers buy, how much and how frequently?
- Can you deliver what they want and when they want it?
- Who else can supply this product or service?
- How strong is this competition?
- Will the market grow or contract?

68

To answer these questions you should:

- Carry out desk research from material published in newspapers, magazines, advertisements and market surveys. You will be surprised how much helpful information is available from the business section of good public libraries and trade associations.
- Visit potential retailers and distributors. Do remember that retailers are always looking for new and improved products so they have an interest in talking to potential new suppliers. In the case of large multiple retailers, talk to retail assistants and ask to see the store manager. When you have talked to a few people at branch level you will be much better prepared to go out and talk to the buyer at head office.
- Visit potential customers both large and small. Remember that in a small company only one person may be involved in the purchasing decision, but in a large company many people may be involved and may need to be influenced. Part of your research will be aimed at finding out how companies are organised to buy your particular product or service.
- Visit competitors. A great deal of information can be obtained from competitors just by asking. Few organisations stop to think whether someone approaching them might be a competitor. In this way you can collect samples, sales brochures and price-lists.
- Visit users and discuss the benefits and deficiencies they associate with your type of product or service. You can also take this opportunity to discuss your particular product.

Such contacts may be made by:

- personal visits, which are the best method;
- telephone, but this method can only be used by a skilled person;
- observation, particularly in the case of a would-be retailer, where traffic flows into the shop are of vital importance in deciding on an appropriate location.

The product or service

It is very easy, and bad business, to think that your new product or service has to be the cheapest. People in business are becoming increasingly aware that non-price factors are very important in designing and developing a product. People buy products for a range of complex rational and irrational reasons of which price is only one. The following list shows some of the non-price factors that should be considered when designing and developing a product:

- the physical attributes of a product;
- its design;
- performance;
- packaging;
- after sales service;
- availability;
- colour, flavour, odour, touch;
- image;
- specification;
- payment terms.

Buyers are less likely to purchase a new product because it is exactly or nearly the same as one already on the market. Somehow you have to distinguish or differentiate your product or service from its competitors. Decide whether potential customers are likely to buy a new product which is better or worse according to each of the characteristics listed above. In doing this, work out which of those characteristics are most important for the particular type of customer at whom you will be aiming.

Identifying a target market

It is very tempting for someone starting up in business to stand on top of a hill looking out over a large city and say to himself or herself, 'Look at all those potential customers out there; I cannot fail to get plenty of customers.' But the truth lies in a very different direction. Most of those customers have very different tastes and requirements and already have a very full choice of products and services. Additionally, you may have only limited resources and it would be very expensive to attempt to sell to all of them. By the time you have approached a small proportion you would have run out of money.

Furthermore, customers have very different ideas about furniture, clothing, cars, and in fact most other types of product. Manufacturers respond by providing a choice of goods and services different from their competitors'. This is called product differentiation. But it would be impossible for every manufacturer to provide a range of goods wide enough to satisfy the needs of all the different types of customer. The way manufacturers solve this problem is to identify a group of customers with similar tastes and requirements and then design a product which meets the needs of that particular group.

Identifying a target market is one of the critical success factors in marketing and is no simple task. In technical marketing jargon it is called market segmentation.

Markets can be segmented in many different ways. They may be segmented, for example, in terms of:

- the size of the business;
- type of business;
- price of the product or service;
- geographical region;
- size and consumption pattern of the users;
- how conservative they are in trying new products or services;
- the length of time taken to make a purchasing decision and the procedure for doing this.

The purpose of market segmentation is to enable the business to identify a group of customers for which its product or service is designed and directed, and to enable it to concentrate its limited resources on marketing and selling to them.

Let us take the example of company XYZ which set up in business to sell a service. The potential for this service lay among solicitors, accountants, banks, merchant banks and industrial companies which needed to retain large volumes of bulky files and other information. The temptation was for company XYZ to aim at all the firms in all these sectors. However, a brief look at the number of firms under each category made it obvious that it would cost too much to write to them all and would take years to follow this up with telephone calls and personal visits. By carrying out a number of personal market research interviews with a selection of firms in each category and of different sizes, company XYZ was able to identify its target of medium-sized firms in one particular category. The target market identified was characterised by:

- being under considerable pressure to define more cost-effective ways of doing things;
- being unable to pass higher costs on in higher fees;
- being less conservative and more adaptable to change than the larger firms;
- having the decision-making process concentrated in the hands of only a few people in contrast to the larger firms where far more people were involved in the purchasing decision.

By identifying this target market, company XYZ was able to concentrate on a relatively small number of potential customers where it obtained sufficient test trials followed by full implementation to build a profitable business. Furthermore, by targeting medium-sized firms in this sector it avoided the mainstream of competition from its large competitors who fought each other over the prize of the even larger ones.

Selling and promotion

Having identified a target market and developed a suitable product or service, the start-up business must decide on the most cost-effective way to reach its target customers. Nowadays companies have an almost unlimited choice of media and other forms of promotion. The choice will depend on a whole range of factors, including the type of product, the number of potential customers in the target group, and the costs and effectiveness of the various methods available. Listed below are 20 of the most common:

- customer sales departments
- sales agents
- telephone sales
- direct mail
- posters
- radio
- TV
- newspapers
- journals
- leaflets and brochures
- mail order
- exhibitions and shows
- party plans
- cinema
- in-store demonstrations
- window displays and showcases
- distribution of product samples
- public relations
- conferences and workshops
- promotion.

In selecting how much a business should spend and which of the above methods to use, the management would be well advised to consult a small advertising agency and/or firm of management consultants.

For example, effective participation in a well-chosen exhibition can work wonders for small, little-known businesses seeking customers. However, common mistakes include choosing an unsuitable exhibition, underestimating the number of people and costs involved, and omitting to follow up on all interested contacts after the exhibition.

In business start-ups and expansion, it is easy to overlook the workload in generating new business. If you should doubt this point, estimate the number of sales leads you need in order to generate one order. For one sale simply estimate:

- how many leads are required to generate one first interview;
- how many contacts with a named, relevant person are needed as a prelude to a first interview;
- how many first interviews you need for making a first sales presentation;
- how many second interviews you need for overcoming objections and confirming details;
- how many third interviews you need in the final bid for the business;
- your likely conversion rate.

If you make a realistic assessment, you should not be surprised if you need over 100 leads to achieve one sale. When you estimate the actual cost in terms of time, you will appreciate the workload in generating new business.

8
Managing the Business

Introduction

An efficiently run business is more likely to succeed than a business where organisation is lacking on the administrative side. In the early stages, it may seem to be an economy to attempt to deal with paperwork yourself in the evenings and at weekends, but if you let things get out of hand it will become a false economy, as your books of account and other tasks fall behind. A good bookkeeper/administrator, perhaps initially on a part-time basis, to deal with the accounting and administrative requirements of the business, is normally a sound investment.

Accounting systems

Legal requirements
The Companies Act 1985 requires that the directors of a limited company ensure that proper books of account are kept with respect to:

- all monies received and paid and the purpose to which they were applied;
- all sales and purchases by the company;
- all assets and liabilities of the company.

They are also required to prepare financial statements on an annual basis and, other than for small businesses, to have these accounts audited by an independent accountant who is a registered auditor.

There are no legal requirements in respect of accounting records for an unincorporated business other than to supply annual financial statements to the Inland Revenue which can be supported by documentary evidence, and the maintenance of the appropriate records for PAYE and VAT purposes if the business is registered. However, in practical terms the accounting requirements of all businesses are similar.

Management requirements

It is important that the proprietors establish a sound and informative accounting system, not only for statutory purposes but also for their own commercial purposes. There is no doubt that the more successful businesses are those where the proprietors are made aware of the company's financial position on a regular basis.

The accounting system

The accounting system adopted by the business should therefore be designed to provide the information and controls required by the Companies Act 1985 (where applicable), HM Customs and Excise (who administer VAT) and the Inland Revenue (for PAYE, income and corporation tax purposes). The sophistication of the system will depend on individual requirements but it will, in any case, establish the flow of documents, and their filing and retrieval within the system. In general, it is advisable to keep your systems as simple and straightforward as possible.

A standard set of books of account would comprise:

- *Cash book* – to record receipts and payments through the bank accounts.
- *Petty cash book* – to record payments of a smaller nature in cash. It is usual for cash receipts to be banked along with cheques.
- *Purchase day book* – an analysed list of invoices from suppliers.
- *Purchase ledger* – a record of the amounts owed to suppliers.
- *Sales day book* – an analysed list of your sales invoices.
- *Sales ledger* – a record of amounts owed by your debtors.
- *Control accounts* – total accounts for the cash and petty cash books and for the sales and purchase ledgers which enable you to double check that all the entries have been made correctly.
- *Wages book / deduction sheets* – individual and total payroll records.
- *Register of fixed assets* – a listing of plant, equipment, cars and other fixed assets to enable their existence and insurance to be controlled.
- *Nominal ledger* – the principal book, in which entries are made in total from other books listed above, and from which accounts are prepared.

The books of account are where the transactions of the business are recorded when the paperwork involved has been processed. Systems are also required for:

- dealing with ordering goods or services, checking their receipt and dealing with the recording and payment of purchase invoices;

- receiving and processing customers' orders, despatching goods, invoicing out sales and receiving payment;
- controlling the workforce and the hours worked;
- controlling the movement of stock; and
- producing regular management information.

Computers

Many of the above books of account can be maintained on a computer, which is worth considering at the outset if you anticipate that large volumes will necessitate this at an early date. It is far easier to set up and become familiar with a computer system while volume is still comparatively small than to transfer large quantities of data later, which can be time-consuming and costly. There are many computer systems on the market which can be expanded as the business grows by adding additional equipment or increasing the capacity of existing equipment without having to discard any of the initial system purchased. Even if you do not use a computer to start with, it may be worth bearing possible computerisation in mind when designing your accounting system, so that the computer (when you get it) will fit into your existing office routines, rather than causing disruption to your staff and the systems that they are used to operating.

Accounting disciplines

Sales invoicing

Prompt invoicing of sales is the first requirement of good cash control. A customer usually takes credit by delaying payment to his supplier and this period will only commence when he approves the invoice.

Banking of cash received

Prompt banking of cash received is the next requirement. All cheques should be banked on the day they are received, as should amounts received in cash. You should avoid using cash receipts to replenish your petty cash or as drawings, as this will eventually catch up with you when you forget to enter it in the accounting system and then chase a customer who has already paid you.

Bank and cash reconciliations

Regular (at least monthly) totalling of your cash books, and reconciliations with bank statements or cash in hand as appropriate, will quickly identify any errors. Regular reconciliations will mean that you rely on the balances shown in your cash books which will help you to monitor your cash flow.

Control accounts
Regular reconciliation of control or total accounts to the list of balances in the appropriate ledgers enables errors to be found more easily, since the error can only have occurred since the last reconciliation. If that was a year ago, tracing the error will be time-consuming!

Credit control
Cash is the lifeblood of any business. The chasing of outstanding debts is one of the most important functions in a business and uses the information in your sales ledger, which must therefore be kept up to date. Efficient credit control will ensure that your cash flow is maintained, and you can continue in business. There is no point in selling goods or services if you do not get paid for them. A telephone call will often suffice to collect a debt from a slow payer, and a 'softly, softly' approach will sometimes be more effective than a threatening letter. However, whatever method you adopt you must keep the pressure on your customers to pay.

Stock control
It is important to implement a stock control system in order to:

- provide details of what is in stock at any period of time;
- identify when stock needs to be reordered;
- identify overstocking, slow-moving or obsolete stock;
- provide information to arrive at the value of your stock for accounting purposes.

Ordering of goods
You need to establish a system for placing orders with suppliers, monitoring the receipt and quality of those goods or services, accounting for the purchase in your books of account and finally paying the invoice.

Filing systems

The basic rules are to open a file when it is needed, and to file all completed paperwork as soon as possible.

Five categories of filing should suffice:

- *Office* – personnel, advertising, insurance, general correspondence.
- *Legal* – contracts, leases etc.

- *Accounting* – purchase and sales invoices, payment vouchers, bank statements etc.
- *Equipment* – plant, office furniture and equipment, motor vehicles.
- *Sales* – customers' correspondence, price-lists, competitors' price-lists etc.

Company administration

The importance of a limited company's statutory records should not be underestimated; they are definitive proof of the company's legal existence and of its memory. The records that should be kept are:

- register of shareholders;
- minutes of directors' and shareholders' meetings;
- register of directors and secretaries;
- register of charges;
- register of directors' interests in shares;
- register of share or stock transfers;
- register of debenture holders;
- copies of directors' service contracts.

Management accounts/budgets

In Chapter 2 the preparation of the business plan to set your objectives and determine the level of finance you require was described. However, this must not be seen as a one-off exercise. Good planning and budgeting are ongoing requirements if the business is to survive and grow.

In order to manage the business effectively you must use the accounting and administrative systems described in this chapter to prepare regular (usually monthly) management accounts and compare these accounts with your original budgets.

Many businesses fail because the management do not have a financial handle on where their business is going. If, for example, your sales are 50 per cent lower than those budgeted, or your expenses are 20 per cent higher than anticipated, then the level of cash you require will increase. Equally, your business might be more successful than originally envisaged. In either case you will probably need to refer back to your bank for additional finance. The bank manager will not be prepared to advance further funds unless he understands fully the position of the business and the exact reasons why the problem has arisen.

It is essential to realise that management accounts are prepared not only for your bank manager/investor but more importantly to enable you to run the business on a day-to-day basis. In Appendix 8 is detailed a simple format for the comparison of monthly accounting information with the budgets prepared by the company. The variances on both a monthly and cumulative basis should be analysed carefully so that you can identify how they have arisen and take corrective action as appropriate.

Most of the items in the monthly accounting package are self-descriptive, but you will need to bear in mind the following.

Depreciation

The assets you purchase to run your business (motor vehicles, plant and machinery etc) have a finite life. It is necessary to write off those assets against your profit and loss account by way of charging depreciation. For example, if you buy a motor van now for £5000 and it has a life of four years, you should charge £1250 to the profit and loss account each year, representing the cost to you of using that vehicle.

Stock

Stock should be valued at the month end at the cost to you. However, if you are not able to sell it at cost (eg it becomes obsolete) then you should value it at realisable value. It may not always be possible to count every item of stock at every month end to determine its value, but it is imperative to make as accurate an assessment as you can on a monthly basis and then verify the figures, say every quarter, by carrying out a full stocktake. Management frequently find that when they are preparing their year end accounts they have been wrongly estimating stocks at month ends and therefore have been obtaining inaccurate information on how the business is going.

Gross profit

When preparing the original budgets you would have determined the mark-up on your goods. The mark-up is the difference between the price at which you sell goods and their cost to you. The extent to which you are achieving your budgeted mark-up can be determined by comparing the percentage relationship between your sales and your gross profit (shown in Appendix 8 as 'gross profit percentage'). If there is a wide divergence between actual and budgeted results, you need to investigate immediately to determine the cause (eg is your sale price correct?; are the goods costing you more than anticipated?; is there an error in your accounting?).

Other overheads

Overheads need to be watched on a regular basis. Many businesses control and achieve their gross profit levels only to have them dissipated by overspending on expenses.

Working capital

You will frequently hear the term 'working capital' which in simple terms is the difference between your current assets and your current liabilities (Appendix 8, balance sheet line D). Current assets are items such as cash plus stock and other assets which will be converted into cash within one year. Current liabilities are debts which are due to be paid within one year.

Break-even

As mentioned earlier in this book, understanding the business's break-even point is a useful management tool. In order to identify the break-even point of the business two further concepts need to be understood:

Variable costs	are those which change depending on the value of sales and production (eg purchase of materials, direct labour costs).
Fixed costs	are those which remain the same whatever the level of sales and production (eg rent, rates, management salaries).

The break-even point is calculated using the formula:

$$\frac{\text{Total fixed costs}}{\text{Selling price} - \text{variable cost per unit}}$$

For example, assume the following figures are extracted from a company's budgets:

	Budget £	Fixed £	Variable £
Sales	200,000	–	200,000
Cost of manufacture	110,000	–	110,000
Cost of distribution	10,000	–	10,000
Cost of selling	30,000	–	30,000
Cost of administration	15,000	15,000	–
Cost of financing	5,000	5,000	–
	170,000	20,000	150,000
Net profit	30,000		

Budgeted sales volume is 10,000 items selling at a price of £20 each.

It is apparent from the above information that the variable cost per unit is:

$$\frac{£150,000}{10,000} = £15 \text{ per unit}$$

Using the formula above the break-even point is:

$$\frac{£20,000 \text{ (total fixed costs)}}{£20 \text{ (selling price)} - £15 \text{ (variable cost per unit)}} = 4,000 \text{ units}$$

Therefore, based on this budget, the business must sell at least 4,000 units at a selling price of £20 each to cover the total costs to the company.

The figures can be proved as follows:

	Budget (10,000 units) £		Break-even (4,000 units) £	
Sales	200,000	(100%)	80,000	(100%)
Variable costs	150,000	(75%)	60,000	(75%)
Contribution to overheads	50,000		20,000	
Fixed overheads	20,000		20,000	
Net profit	30,000		Nil	

- the percentage relationship between sales and variable costs is the same for the budget and break-even results.

Conclusion

Many people running businesses concentrate on the selling and production side and give no thought to the financial implications of what they are doing. A good accounting and administration system will give you the management tools to make valid business decisions and help your business grow.

Auditors/accountants

Limited companies

Under the Companies Act 1985 a limited company is required to have its accounts audited on an annual basis by an independent accountant. Companies with a turnover of £90,000 or less are not required to have an audit. Certain companies with a turnover of between £90,001 and £350,000 per annum are exempt from audit but instead need an independent accountant's report. The auditor is required to review the accounts and the systems used, and to state whether these accounts give 'a true and fair view' of the state of affairs and results of the business at a point in time.

Sole traders/Partnerships
In relation to sole traders and partnerships an accountant is usually engaged to prepare periodic (annual) accounts.

For all business entities it is usual for the accountant to deal on behalf of the business with the Inland Revenue to agree corporation and/or income tax liabilities.

General advice
It is important that you obtain sound professional advice at the outset of your business. It is likely that the accountant will have been involved in assisting you in preparing your business plan but you should seek advice, among other things, on:

- the bookkeeping system most appropriate to your circumstances;
- VAT and PAYE registration and systems;
- preparation of regular management information and interpretation of results;
- general business matters.

9
Providing for the Future

Introduction

Whether an individual is in business as a sole trader, in partnership or is running a limited company it is important to plan a pension for the future. It is worth bearing in mind that a male retiring at the age of 60 has an average life expectancy of approximately 21 years. A pension will therefore be expected to provide an adequate level of income for approximately a quarter of a person's lifetime. In short, a pension is the most important investment an individual will make apart from his or her own business.

The tax and legal framework governing pension provision, for the self-employed and those in employment where no pension is provided, differs from that for employees provided with pensions by their employers. The legislation in relation to pensions has been changed substantially in the last five years. Sound, independent professional advice is essential before entering into any pension arrangements.

Pension provision

The following provisions are for the self-employed and those not provided with a pension by their employers.

Personal pension schemes

Individuals who are self-employed or are not provided with a pension by their employer may invest a proportion of their net relevant earnings (ie earnings after the expenses of the business but before personal tax allowances or tax have been deducted). Up to the age of 35 this proportion is 17.5 per cent and it increases with age to a maximum of 40 per cent for individuals aged between 61 and 74. Personal pension schemes superseded, from 1 July 1988, what used to be called retirement annuity policies (RAPs). Anyone who has an RAP should take professional advice before changing his or her pension arrangements. Under the personal pension scheme legislation, banks, building societies and unit trust groups may also market personal pension schemes in addition to life assurance companies, subject to compliance with the legislation.

The premiums paid (up to the statutory limits) are deductible from income for tax purposes and, once invested, accumulate in a preferentially taxed fund. At retirement you may take up to 25 per cent of the accumulated fund as a tax-free cash sum and use the balance of the fund to purchase a pension which will be taxed under PAYE. You may take the benefits at any age from 50 onwards and need not retire in order to do so. The latest age at which benefits may be taken is 75.

The purpose of paying personal pension scheme premiums is to provide a pension on retirement where the premiums are invested in an investment scheme which enjoys substantial tax benefits as outlined above.

Types of policy
There are four broad categories of scheme in which you can invest:

- *Non-profit policies* which give a guaranteed return unaffected by future investment conditions. These are now rarely used but may possibly be of benefit for people very near to retirement with little time for their investment to grow.
- *With profit policies* which operate on the basis of profits or bonuses being added at periodic intervals which, once added, form part of the policy. In addition further bonuses are usually payable at the date benefits are taken to reflect investment returns over the term of the policy.
- *Unit-linked policies* where the premium paid by the individual purchases units in one of a range of funds offered by the personal pension scheme provider. Once invested, the unit values reflect the underlying value of the funds in which they are invested.
- *Deposit administration policies* which work on the basis that premiums are invested in a deposit fund often linked to fixed interest rates or building society lending rates.

Individual circumstances will dictate what type of policy or combination of policies is likely to be most appropriate, though it is usual for most people to effect a combination of with profit and unit-linked policies.

For employees, pension benefits are as follows:

Retirement benefit schemes
An employer may provide pension benefits for employees by setting up a scheme which provides:

- a maximum of two-thirds of the final salary as long as the employee has at least 20 years' service and subject to a maximum pension of £51,200, ie two-thirds of £76,800 (which is now the upper limit for exempt approved schemes following the Finance Act 1989). The £76,800 earnings limit is increased annually by the Retail Price Index, rising to £78,600 for the year 1995/96;

- a maximum spouse's pension of two-thirds of the employee's pension payable to the spouse or dependant, in the event of predeceasing the spouse after retirement;

- lump sum life assurance cover of up to four times the salary at the date of death (subject to prevailing earnings limit) if an employee dies before retirement (1992/93 maximum £307,200, rising to £314,400 in 1995/96);

- spouse's and dependant's pensions of up to four-ninths of the employee's salary at the date of death if he or she dies before retirement.

Payments in respect of the above will often be made by the employer to a life assurance company if the scheme has less than, say, 150 to 200 members; the employee may contribute up to 15 per cent of salary by way of ordinary and Additional Voluntary Contributions (AVCs) and obtain tax relief at his or her highest marginal rate. Employees may pay Free Standing AVCs (FSAVCs) to pension providers of their own choice subject again to a 15 per cent of salary limit, including contributions to their employer's scheme.

Personal pension schemes

As an alternative, an employer can contribute to an employee's personal pension scheme. The contribution limits (17.5 to 40 per cent depending on age) apply whether contributions are made by the employer or employee alone or in combination. Payments cannot be made to personal pensions by members of a company pension scheme.

Small self-administered pension schemes

The employer may also consider establishing a small self-administered pension scheme (SSAS) for the directors and senior executives of the company. Under this type of scheme (for firms which must have fewer than 12 members) the company pays premiums to the SSAS and these funds are then invested for the benefit of the members of the scheme (ie the employees, including directors) and can be invested in a range of approved assets such as equities and commercial property as well as insurance company funds, or held as cash. The maximum benefits are the same as for employees in a retirement benefits scheme.

Loan facilities

Based on monies paid into a fund and anticipated benefits, the employee may obtain loan facilities. This is particularly useful in respect of mortgages which can be linked to pension premiums being paid. It is important to note that the policy or plan cannot under law be assigned. Instead, the lender accepts the pension plan as evidence of the ability to repay the mortgage at retirement. The lender will still usually require an assignment over a life assurance policy in order to ensure that the loan is repaid in the event of death before retirement. A charge over the property will also be required in the normal way.

Trustee investments and corporate borrowings

Inland Revenue legislation allows the trustees of particular types of company pension scheme, particularly SSASs, to loan funds back to the company and to purchase, either directly or with the assistance of a mortgage, commercial property which can subsequently be leased to the company. There are strict rules imposed by the Inland Revenue controlling such transactions, particularly to protect members' benefits, and specialist independent advice should be sought.

Previous pension rights

You may have retained pension benefits within a previous employer's scheme, or your own personal pension or Retirement Annuity Plan. It is important to take these benefits, and any anticipated State pension benefits into account when working out your future pension provisions. While consolidating your funds into personal arrangements may be considered, you should carefully consider the potential loss of guarantees offered by company pension schemes, and if in doubt, seek specialist independent advice.

Conclusion

In summary, planning can provide for an individual, together with his or her spouse and dependants, not only a pension during retirement but also valuable life benefits payable on death before retirement. In addition, the tax-free cash sum may be used to obtain tax-efficient personal mortgage facilities, and the investment flexibility offered by small company schemes may offer a business additional financial assistance.

For these reasons any person in business should give serious consideration to making appropriate pension arrangements at an early age.

10
Obtaining Assistance

A large number of people and professional bodies are able to give advice and assistance to small growing businesses. It is common sense to use an outsider for a particular matter when your business needs that expertise but is not able to have a suitable person on the payroll.

The proprietor will often attempt to cover too many areas, spending a disproportionate amount of time on one thing to the detriment of the enterprise as a whole. This chapter, therefore, highlights some of the help and advice available. Appendix 9 lists a selection of the names, addresses and telephone numbers of those who are available to help you.

Accountants

In many small businesses, the accountant comes once a year to prepare annual accounts, and audit them if they are for a company. The only other time an accountant will be contacted will be if the business is in difficulties, either with the VAT or tax authorities, or with the bank.

There are, however, a wide range of other services which are available from firms of accountants. These include:

- advice on the best type of trading entity for your business, taking into account your own personal circumstances and any legal or professional requirements;
- organising the legal registration of a company or advising on a partnership agreement;
- designing and setting up suitable accounting and bookkeeping systems for the business and helping to monitor the information;
- writing up the books (or processing the accounting information on computer);
- dealing with payroll preparation and annual PAYE returns;
- assisting in the preparation of budgets and cash flow forecasts for

internal use as well as in connection with applications for bank facilities, and attending meetings with your bank manager;

- advising on possible sources of finance, and helping with the preparation of a business plan to achieve the financing required;
- advising on grants available when setting up or expanding your business;
- advising on the taxation aspects of your business and dealing with the Inland Revenue as agent on all matters to do with taxation.

Different firms of accountants have different services to offer, and it is advisable to look around at several before choosing one to use. It is also worth bearing in mind that a larger firm will probably have greater expertise, whereas a smaller firm will probably offer a more personal service.

Solicitors

In a practical sense your accountant and lawyer will often work together to assist you. Solicitors will be able to offer you advice on:

Structure
When you have decided, in conjunction with your accountant, what legal form your business should take, a solicitor should be consulted if anything out of the ordinary is required: for instance, a company with different types of share capital or a partnership where a written agreement is needed to formalise the arrangements.

Property
Almost all firms of solicitors have expertise in property matters, and assistance with understanding contracts and leases is essential, particularly in determining your liability with regard to dilapidations, repairs and improvements.

Trading contracts
Many businesses do not require formal contracts with their customers, but even the terms of trade printed on your documentation can constitute a legal contract, and it is as well to ensure that these are checked by a solicitor. For businesses with complicated delivery dates and payment arrangements, it is even more important that the contract should be legally watertight.

Debt collection
A solicitor's letter to a slow payer will often lead to recovery of the debt,

but this course should only be followed where others have failed and if you are prepared to take the debtor to court if necessary. Using solicitors for debt collection can be expensive, and is not an alternative to efficient credit control. If you frequently require a debt collection service, there are specialist agencies whose names are in the local library, Yellow Pages and Citizens' Advice Bureau.

Litigation
If you need to sue someone, or are yourself sued, you will need the specialist services of a solicitor and also, in many instances, a barrister. Taking a case to court is very expensive, and a great number of cases are settled out of court by agreement between the parties through their lawyers.

Employment
Employment law is complex and advice should be sought, particularly in relation to contracts of service and dismissal procedures.

Other matters
Other matters which may require specialist legal advice are patents, franchises, foreign law and insolvency.

The Law Society
The Law Society has lists of solicitors on a regional basis. Recommendations from colleagues, friends, your bank manager or accountant may also be useful. It is quite usual for people to use different firms for different types of work, depending on the experience and expertise required.

Bank manager

Your bank manager is an excellent source of general business advice. The experience and accessibility of the bank manager is an important criterion in choosing a bank.

In addition, some banks have set up special departments offering services to businesses. Each bank has a different way of dealing with the matter, but all have booklets setting out what facilities they have on offer to attract customers. Many of these booklets are aimed at the person wishing to set up in business.

In general, the more your bank manager knows about you and your business, the more likely he will be able to assist with your financial requirements. Regular meetings and the provision of regular financial information to your manager will help to identify when you will need increased facilities or a loan from the bank, so that the necessary arrangements can be made in advance.

If a cash flow crisis develops unexpectedly, the manager is likely to be more sympathetic and helpful to a well-organised and forward-looking customer than to one whose business lurches from crisis to crisis.

Business Links

Under the auspices of the DTI, the Government has encouraged the establishment of 'Business Links' which are a 'network of independent local business information and advice centres offering a wide range of services to the business community, designed to enhance the competitiveness of local companies. They are run by partnerships which include Chambers of Commerce, Training and Enterprise Councils, local authorities, Enterprise Agencies and the Department of Trade and Industry. They will be the places to access a full range of business support services.' (Quoted from *Business Link Questions and Answers* Issue 1.)

Business Links will concentrate on services such as:

● support from personal business advisers;
● export services;
● business health checks;
● quality and design services;
● business skills courses;
● business start-up.

The services will be available to all businesses in the locality of the Business Link and will concentrate particularly on small businesses with growth potential.

It is anticipated that by the end of 1995 every company in England will have access to a Business Link. Included in Appendix 9 is a list of DTI Government Office contact numbers where you can enquire about your nearest Business Link.

Scotland, Wales and Northern Ireland do not have Business Links. Your local DTI office will be able to tell you what assistance is available in these countries.

Appendices

Appendix 1

Business Plan: Suggested Contents

1. EXECUTIVE SUMMARY
2. CORPORATE OBJECTIVES
3. HISTORY
4. PRODUCTS OR SERVICES
5. MARKET AND MARKET STRATEGY
    (a) customers;
    (b) market size and trends;
    (c) competition;
    (d) estimated market share;
    (e) market strategy.
6. RESEARCH AND DEVELOPMENT
7. MANAGEMENT
8. BASIS OF OPERATION
9. FINANCIAL INFORMATION
10. FINANCE REQUIRED AND ITS APPLICATION
11. PRINCIPAL RISKS AND PROBLEMS
12. LONGER-TERM OBJECTIVES

Appendices

A. DETAILED PROJECTIONS
B. ASSUMPTIONS
C. MANAGEMENT
D. PRODUCT LITERATURE ETC

Appendix 2

Specimen Budget for the year ending...

All in £000s		Jan	Feb	March	April
Sales	A				
Less:					
Cost of sales (opening stock plus purchases less closing stock)	B				
Gross profit (A–B)	C				
Gross profit % (C/A × 100%)					
Overheads					
Salaries and wages					
Directors' remuneration					
Depreciation					
Light, heat and power					
Repairs and renewals					
Rent and rates					
Travelling and entertaining					
Advertising					
Bank interest and charges					
General expenses					
Total overheads	D				
Net profit (C–D)	E				
Net profit % (E/A × 100%)					

May	June	July	Aug	Sept	Oct	Nov	Dec	Total

Appendix 3

Specimen Cash Flow for the year ending...

All in £000s		Jan	Feb	March	April
Receipts					
Sales					
Sundry receipts					
	A				
Payments					
Purchases					
Employees' salaries and wages					
Directors' remuneration					
PAYE					
VAT					
Rent and rates					
Light, heat and power					
Repairs and renewals					
Travelling and entertaining					
Bank interest and charges					
Advertising					
General expenses					
	B				
Net inflow/(outflow) (A–B)					
Balance at beginning of month					
Balance at end of month					

May	*June*	*July*	*Aug*	*Sept*	*Oct*	*Nov*	*Dec*	*Total*

Appendix 4

Specimen Balance Sheets at month end...

All in £000s		Jan	Feb	March	April
FIXED ASSETS Freehold/leasehold property Plant and machinery, motor vehicles					
	A				
CURRENT ASSETS Stock and work in progress Debtors Cash at bank and in hand					
	B				
CURRENT LIABILITIES Creditors Bank overdraft					
	C				
NET CURRENT ASSETS (B–C)	D				
LIABILITIES PAYABLE IN MORE THAN ONE YEAR	E				
NET ASSETS (A+D–E)	F				
Share capital/ Proprietor's undrawn profit Profit retained in the business					
Note that F=G	G				

May	June	July	Aug	Sept	Oct	Nov	Dec	

Appendix 5

Main Forms Used for PAYE/NIC Purposes

Form P11 (Deductions working sheet)

The deductions working sheet is used to record for each employee details of pay, tax, National Insurance contributions, Statutory Sick Pay and Statutory Maternity Pay for each period during a tax year.

It is most important that amended codes are noted on the deductions working sheet as soon as they are received from the PAYE tax office to ensure that they are implemented for the next pay period.

Form P46 (Particulars of employee for whom no code has been notified to the employer)

Form P46 should be completed if either:

    (a) a new employee does not produce a Form P45; or

    (b) the pay of an existing employee rises above the PAYE threshold.

The P46 procedure is a vital part of the Inland Revenue's effort to deal with the black economy. It is understood that on their visits to employers PAYE audit teams have instructions to ensure that Form P46 has been completed where necessary.

The Inland Revenue do not consider that completing a Form P46 retrospectively frees the employer from liability. If, therefore, the employee has been paid emoluments without deducting tax, the employer is liable to account for tax at the basic rate on the emoluments paid.

Form P15 (Coding claim)

Form P15 is used to provide the Inland Revenue with the information necessary to enable them to issue a notice of coding so that the correct amount of tax is deducted under the PAYE scheme from the employee's remuneration during the tax year. It is only needed when this is the employee's first employment or when he or she cannot produce a Form P45 from his or her previous employment.

Form P45 (Details of employee leaving)

Form P45 is used to summarise details of an employee's pay and tax deducted up to the date of leaving the employment, as detailed on the employer's deductions working sheet, Form P11. The form does not require any details of National Insurance contributions, or Statutory Sick Pay – these details are subsequently included on Form P14 (see below).

If the employer makes payments to the employee after Form P45 has been issued, tax should be deducted at the basic rate from the full amount with no relief for allowances etc. Details of such payments should be included on Form P14.

There are no provisions enabling employers to use substitute Forms P45, although employers with computerised payroll systems may use Forms P45 (continuous) which have been adapted for use with such systems. If an employer wishes to adopt this procedure, he or she should contact the local PAYE tax office.

The employer is not allowed to issue a duplicate Form P45 to an employee who loses the form. It will be necessary in these circumstances for the new employer to use the P46 procedure.

A retiring employee is treated as ceasing employment and a Form P45 should be issued, except where the retiring employee is to receive a pension from the employer. (In that case, Form P160 should be completed.) Note that this does not extend to pensions from the employer's pension scheme where a Form P45 should be completed in the usual way.

Forms P14, P60 (End of year return and employer's certificate: pay, tax and National Insurance contributions)

This form is a three-part form – a top copy and two carbon copies. Part 1 (the DSS copy) and Part 2 (the Inland Revenue copy) – which together comprise Form P14 – are submitted to the Collector of Taxes. Part 3 of the form constitutes Form P60 which is handed to the employee.

The forms summarise the pay, tax and National Insurance contributions and Statutory Sick Pay details for each employee for the tax year.

Many employers operate a mechanised or computer-based salaries or wages system. Such employers may seek Inland Revenue approval for the use of a substitute pre-printed three-part document. If the employer wishes to adopt this system rather than use the Inland Revenue forms, he or she should contact the local PAYE tax office.

Form P35 (Employer's annual statement)

Form P35 is used to summarise for the Inland Revenue details of tax, National Insurance contributions, Statutory Sick Pay and Statutory Maternity Pay for each employee in a tax year, and also to provide certain specific information relating to employees and others.

It should be noted that Form P35 has been designed to highlight likely weaknesses in the employer's PAYE system, and you should be aware that the Inland Revenue PAYE audit section may be alerted to any weaknesses.

Appendix 6

Specimen Statement of Terms and Conditions of Employment

In accordance with the requirements of the Trade Union Reform & Employment Rights Act 1993 (TURERA 93) this principal statement sets out the main terms and conditions of your employment. Please sign and return the copy of this statement.

Name: ....

Name of employer: ....

Date of commencement: ....

Date of commencement of continuous employment (if different from above):

....

Date of termination of employment (if your employment is for a fixed term):

....

Job title/position: ....
(as a term of your employment, you may be required from time to time and within reason to vary the duties this position entails).

Current salary: £ .... a year/week/hour (delete as applicable). Payable monthly in arrears by credit transfer.

Hours of work: Your normal working hours are .... a week, but you are expected to work such additional hours as may be necessary for the efficient performance of your duties.

Place of work: Your normal place of work is .... As a term of your employment you may be required from time to time to work at a different location, at the reasonable discretion of your employer.

Overtime: All staff except those of manager grade and their equivalent are eligible to receive authorised overtime pay. Hourly overtime pay is calculated by dividing your annual salary by 261 working days in a year, dividing that daily rate by the number of hours worked in a day and multiplying the resultant hourly rate by

1.25. Hourly overtime pay is paid at the discretion of the management and compensatory leave may be granted in lieu.

Holidays: In addition to statutory holidays, you are entitled to .... working days holiday in each year. For any period of service of less than a full holiday year, your entitlement for that year will be calculated by dividing your entitlement by 12 and multiplying that monthly entitlement by your number of complete months of service in that year, rounded to the nearest whole number of days. On leaving employment in the course of the holiday year, any holiday entitlement not taken will be paid to you at the daily rate calculated by dividing your annual salary on your last day of employment by the normal number of days worked each year (261 for full-time staff). If you have exceeded your holiday entitlement on your date of leaving, a deduction will be made from your final payment of the appropriate number of days' pay. For the avoidance of doubt, if you are paid in lieu of notice, you will not be entitled to any additional holiday pay which would otherwise have accrued during your notice period.

Sickness and injury: The policies and procedures relating to absence and payment in the event of sickness are as follows:

[Complete according to your particular circumstances]

Pension and the SERPS: Your entitlement to join the firm's pension scheme are as follows:

[Complete according to your particular circumstances]

Discipline and grievances: The disciplinary rules and grievance procedures relating to your employment are as follows:

[Complete according to your particular circumstances]

Any breach of the disciplinary rules will render you liable to disciplinary action, or summary dismissal for offences of gross misconduct. If you have a grievance or problem arising from your employment, you must follow the procedure in the Employment Manual.

Termination of employment: The periods of notice which you are obliged to give and entitled to receive are set out below:

Staff category	1st year of employment		After 1 year of employment	
	Obliged to give	Entitled to receive	Obliged to give	Entitled to receive
Senior staff	1 month	1 month	3 months	3 months
Junior staff	1 month	1 month	1 month	1 month

The law requires a minimum period of notice of one week for every year of service after two years' service and up to 12 years' service ie minimum of 12 weeks' notice after 12 years' service.

Amendments: Changes to any terms and conditions in this principal statement will be notified to you in writing.

Signed: .... Date: ....
(Signature of employee)

Appendix 7

Statutory Rights of Employees

Statutory rights as provided by the Trade Union Reform and Employment Rights Act 1993, the Race Relations Act 1976, and the Sex Discrimination Act 1976, (Equal Pay Act 1970).

Period of continuous service after which the statutory right takes effect*	Employee's statutory right
Pre-employment	Discrimination – the right to be afforded equal access to employment regardless of sex, race or marital status.
On commencement of employment	The right not to be unlawfully discriminated against in employment on the grounds of sex, race or marital status. The right to receive a Principal Statement of Terms and Conditions of Employment within two months. The right to receive an itemised pay statement (ie gross pay, PAYE, NI etc). The right not to have unlawful deductions made from wages or salaries. The right not to be dismissed or have action short of dismissal taken against you for: a) being or refusing to be a member of an independent trade union; b) taking part in the activities of an independent trade union; c) pregnancy.

Period of continuous service after which the statutory right takes effect*	Employee's statutory right
	The right to reasonable time off to carry out: a) trade union duties – paid; b) trade union activities – unpaid; c) public duties – unpaid; d) anti-natal care – paid; The right of access to data held on computer of which the employee is the subject and the right to seek compensation for damages caused by the loss, destruction or unauthorised disclosure of data, or by inaccurate data. The right to 14 weeks' basic maternity leave with the right to return to work after the baby's birth.**
After one month	The right to receive a Guarantee Payment for up to five days when an employer is unable to provide work in any three month period. The right to receive up to 26 weeks' statutory sick pay if the employee is suspended from work on medical grounds. On termination of employment by the employer, an employee is entitled to receive one week's paid notice.
After 6 months (26 weeks)	If dismissed, the right to receive a written statement of the reason for dismissal. The right to receive statutory maternity pay.
After 2 years (or 5 years for employees working at least 8 hours but less than 16 hours a week)	The right to 40 weeks' maternity leave. The employee's paid notice entitlement increases to one week for each full year of employment, to a maximum of 12 weeks. The right not to be unfairly dismissed.

Period of continuous service after which the statutory right takes effect*	Employee's statutory right
	The right to statutory redundancy pay if the employer's requirement for an employee to carry out work of a particular kind ceases or diminishes.

* A week during which an employee is employed under a contract of employment for more than 16 hours per week counts towards continuous service.

** Subject to certain other conditions being met.

Appendix 8

Specimen Management Accounts

Profit and Loss Account Month ....

		Budget £	Month Actual £	Variance £	Budget £	Cumulative Actual £	Variance £
Sales	A	——	——	——	——	——	——
Opening stock							
Add:							
Purchases							
Less:							
Closing stock							
		——	——	——	——	——	——
Cost of sales	B						
		——	——	——	——	——	——
Gross profit (A–B)	C						
Gross profit % (C/A × 100%)							
Overheads							
Salaries and wages							
Directors' remuneration							
Depreciation							
Light, heat and power							
Repairs and renewals							
Rent and rates							
Travelling and entertaining							
Bank interest and charges							
Advertising							
General expenses							
		——	——	——	——	——	——
Total overheads	D						
		——	——	——	——	——	——
Net profit (C–D)	E						
		══	══	══	══	══	══
Net profit % (E/A × 100%)							

Balance Sheet Month End ....

		Budget £	Actual £	Variance £
FIXED ASSETS				
Freehold/leasehold property				
Motor vehicles				
Plant and machinery				
		___	___	___
Less:				
Depreciation				
		___	___	___
	A			
		___	___	___
CURRENT ASSETS				
Stock and work in progress				
Debtors				
Cash at bank and in hand				
		___	___	___
	B			
		___	___	___
CURRENT LIABILITIES				
Creditors				
Bank overdraft				
		___	___	___
	C			
		___	___	___
NET CURRENT ASSETS (B–C)	D			
LIABILITIES PAYABLE IN MORE THAN ONE YEAR				
(eg bank loans)	E			
		___	___	___
NET ASSETS (A+D–E)	F			
		═══	═══	═══
Representing:				
Share capital/				
Proprietors' undrawn profit				
Profit retained in the business				
		___	___	___
SHAREHOLDERS'/ PROPRIETORS' FUNDS	G			
		═══	═══	═══

[Note that F=G]

Cash Flow for the Month ....

	Budget		Actual	
	£	£	£	£

Balance at the beginning of the month
Add:

Receipts: Sales
             Sundry receipts
             Other (specify)

Less:

Payments:
Purchases
Directors' remuneration
Employees' salaries and wages
PAYE
VAT
Light, heat and power
Repairs and renewals
Rent and rates
Travelling and entertaining
Bank interest and charges
Advertising
General expenses
Capital expenditure
Other (specify)

Balance at the end of the month   £   £

Note: variances between actual and budget for the profit and loss account, balance sheet and cash flow should be analysed in order to effectively run the business.

Appendix 9

Useful Contacts and Addresses

1. Accountants
The Chartered Association of Certified Accountants
29 Lincoln's Inn Fields
London WC2A 3EE
0171 242 6855

The Chartered Institute of Management Accountants
63 Portland Place
London W1N 4AB
0171 637 2311

The Institute of Chartered Accountants in England and Wales
Gloucester House
399 Silbury Boulevard
Central Milton Keynes MK9 2HL
01908 248100

The Institute of Chartered Accountants in Ireland
Chartered Accountants House
87–89 Pembroke Road
Dublin 4
Dublin 680400

The Institute of Chartered Accountants of Scotland
27 Queen Street
Edinburgh EH2 1LA
0131 225 5673

2. Solicitors
The Law Society
113 Chancery Lane
London WC2A 1PL
0171 242 1222

3. Banks

Barclays Bank plc
54 Lombard Street
London EC3P 3AH
0171 621 4000

Lloyds Bank plc
71 Lombard Street
London EC3P 3BS
0171 626 1500

Midland Bank plc
27–32 Poultry
London EC2P 2BX
0171 260 8000

National Westminster Bank plc
21 Lombard Street
London EC3P 3AR
0171 280 4444

The Royal Bank of Scotland plc
67 Lombard Street
London EC3P 3DL
0171 623 4356

Trustee Savings Bank plc
Retail Banking and Insurance
PO Box 6000
Victoria House
Victoria Square
Birmingham B1 1BZ
0121 600 6000

Allied Irish Banks plc
12 Old Jewry
London EC2R 8DP
0171 606 4900

Co-operative Bank plc
80 Cornhill
London EC3V 3NJ
0171 626 4953

National Girobank
10 Milk Street
London EC2V 8JH
0171 600 6020

Chartered Institute of Bankers
10 Lombard Street
London EC3V 9AS
0171 623 3531

4. Local Authorities
From your local telephone book

5. Rural Development Commission
141 Castle Street
Salisbury
Wiltshire SP1 3TP
01722 336255

Also:

The Rural Development Commission
Dacre House
19 Dacre Street
London SW1H 0DH
0171 340 2900

6. Regional Development and Inward Investment Division
Department of Trade and Industry
Regional Selective Assistance
Kingsgate House
66–74 Victoria Street
London SW1E 6SW
0171 215 2565

Or see your local telephone directory

7. Small Firms Service
Contact your local Training and Enterprise Council.

8. English Partnerships
St George's House
Kingsway
Team Valley
Gateshead
Tyne and Wear NE11 0NA
0191 487 8941

9. New Towns

Commission for the New Towns
Glen House
Stag Place
London SW1E 5AJ
0171 828 7722

10. Urban Development Corporations

Black Country Development Corporation
Black Country House
Round Green Road
Oldbury
West Midlands B69 2DG
0121 511 2000

Bristol Development Corporation
2nd Floor
Techno House
Redcliffe Way
Bristol BS1 6NL
0117 9255222

Central Manchester Development Corporation
Churchgate House
56 Oxford Street
Manchester M1 6EU
0161 236 1166

Teesside Development Corporation
Dunedin House
Riverside Quay
Stockton on Tees
Cleveland TS17 6BJ
01642 677123

Leeds Development Corporation
5th Floor, South Point
South Accommodation Road
Leeds LS10 1WP
01132 446273

London Docklands Development Corporation
Thames Quay
191 Marsh Wall
London E14 9TJ
0171 512 3000

Merseyside Development Corporation
Fourth Floor
Royal Liver Building
Pier Head
Liverpool L3 1JH
0151 236 6090

Sheffield Development Corporation
Don Valley House
Savile Street East
Sheffield S4 7UQ
01142 720100

Trafford Park Development Corporation
Trafford Wharf Road
Trafford Park
Manchester M17 1EX
0161 848 8000

Tyne and Wear Development Corporation
Scotswood House
Newcastle Business Park
Newcastle Upon Tyne NE4 7YL
0191 226 1234

11. Freeports
Belfast Airport
Northern Ireland Airports Ltd
Belfast

International Airport
Belfast BT29 4AB
018494 22888 (Ext 3027)

Birmingham Airport
West Midlands Freeport Ltd
Birmingham Airport
Coventry Road
Birmingham B26 3QD
0121 782 0103

Freeport Scotland Ltd
Burns House
Burns Statue Square
Ayr KA7 1UT
01292 281511

Liverpool Port
Mersey Docks and Harbour Co
Maritime Centre
Port of Liverpool
Liverpool L21 1LA
0151 949 6000 or 0151 949 6391 (direct line)

Southampton Free Trade Zone Ltd
Southampton Free Trade Zone
Southampton SO15 1HJ
01703 335995

12. Enterprise Agencies

For details of your Local Enterprise Agency contact:

Business in the Community
8 Stratton Street
London W1X 6AB
0171 629 1600

Scottish Business in the Community
Romano House
43 Station Road
Edinburgh EH12 7AF
0131 334 9876

13. Chambers of Commerce

For details of your local Chamber of Commerce contact:

Association of British Chambers of Commerce:
9 Tufton Street
London SW1P 3QB
0171 222 1555

14. The Training Agency

London Business School
Sussex Place
Regent's Park
London NW1 4SA
0171 262 5050

London and South East Employment Service
236 Gray's Inn Road
London WC1X 8HL
0171 211 4242

15. Business Start-up Scheme

Your local Enterprise Agency or via the local Jobcentre

16. Advertising
Advertising Association
Abford House
15 Wilton Road
London SW1V 1NJ
0171 828 2771

17. Market research
Export Market Information Centre
Department of Trade and Industry
Ashdown House
123 Victoria Street
London SW1E 6RB
0171 215 5444

18. Exporting
British Exporters Association
16 Dartmouth Street
London SW1H 9BL
0171 222 5419

British Overseas Trade Board
Department of Trade and Industry
Ashdown House
123 Victoria Street
London SW1E 6RB
0171 215 5000

(Or nearest BOTB regional office)

Export Credits Guarantee Department
2 Exchange Tower
Harbour Exchange Square
London E14 9GS
0171 512 7000

Institute of Export
64 Clifton Street
London EC2A 4HB
0171 247 9812

Technical Help for Exporters
389 Chiswick High Road
London W4 4AL
0181 996 7111

19. Europe
Liaison Office for the UK
European Investment Bank
68 Pall Mall
London SW1Y 5ES
0171 839 3351

European Coal and Steel Community
The Directorate of Credit and Investments
Commission of European Communities
Bâtiment Jean Monnet
Kirchberg, L2920
Luxembourg
010 352 43011

20. Enterprise Zones
General information:

Department of the Environment
2 Marsham Street
London SW1P 3EB
0171 276 6166

21. Venture capital
British Venture Capital Association
Essex House
12–13 Essex Street
London WC2R 3AA
0171 240 3846

22. Department of Trade and Industry
Regional Telephone numbers for advice on innovation, investment, exports and
other help:

London 0171 215 5000
North East 0191 232 4722
East Midlands 01602 506181
North West 0161 952 4000
South East 0171 215 0572
South West 01272 272666
West Midlands 0121 212 5000
Yorkshire and Humberside 01532 443171
Scotland 0141-248 4774
Wales 01223 825111
Northern Ireland 01212 529900
Small businesses 0800 222999

23. ACAS
Advisory Conciliation and Arbitration Service
Clifton House
83–117 Euston Road
London NW1 2RB
0171 396 5100 (public enquiry line)

Head Office
27 Wilton Street
London SW1X 7AZ
0171 210 3613

24. Patents
Chartered Institute of Patent Agents
Staple Inn Buildings
High Holborn
London WC1V 7PZ
0171 405 9450

25. Limited company information, formation and searches
Companies House
Crown Way
Maindy
Cardiff CF4 3UZ
01222 380801

Companies House
100 George Street
Edinburgh EH2 3DJ
0131 225 5774

Industrial Development Board
IDB House
64 Chichester Street
Belfast BT1 4JX
01232 234488

London Search Room
Companies House
55–71 City Road
London EC1Y 1BB
0171 253 9393

Or most Company Registration Agents from the Yellow Pages

26. Factoring
Association of British Factors and Discounters
1 Northumberland Avenue
London WC2N 5BW
0171 930 9112

27. Franchising
The British Franchise Association
Thames View
Newtown Road
Henley on Thames
Oxon RG9 1HG
01491 578049

28. DTI Business Link contact numbers

Office	Number
North West	0161 236 2171
Yorkshire & Humberside	0113 244 3171
East Midlands	0115 950 6181
South East	0171 215 5000
East	0122 346 1939
Merseyside	0151 227 4111
South West	0117 927 2666
West Midlands	0121 212 5000
North East	0191 232 4722

Further Reading from Kogan Page

Kogan Page publish an extensive list of books for small and medium-sized businesses. A full list of titles is available from Kogan Page at 120 Pentonville Road, London N1 9JN; Telephone 0171 278 0433; Fax 0171 837 6348.

Index